D1128308

TIME

ALEXANDER HAMILTON

A Founding Father's Visionary Genius—and His Tragic Fate

A CENTRAL FIGURE *From humble beginnings, Alexander Hamilton grew to play a crucial role in laying the groundwork for the United States of America.*

CONTENTS

A Hamilton

THE VISION AND PASSION OF A COMPLICATED FOUNDER

BY JOANNE B. FREEMAN

ALEXANDER HAMILTON IS A PROBlematic Founder. A power and a prodigy with a self-destructive streak, he was a notoriously difficult man of extremes. Always sure that he was right, he charged headfirst into battles with nary a look back, sometimes with disastrous results. Desperate to make a name for himself and equally desperate to destroy defamers of that name, he entangled himself in countless disputes; he was involved in 10 affairs of honor before his fatal duel with Aaron Burr. Powerhouse that he was, Hamilton was often his own worst enemy.

Yet there's no denying his Founder status; he had an enormous shaping influence on the young United States. A fervent nationalist and the country's first secretary of the Treasury, he brought order to the new republic's finances, earned it credit at home and abroad and strengthened the national government, setting constitutional precedents that persist today.

To some degree, Hamilton's policies and personality were of a piece. He dedicated his considerable energies to the establishment of energetic governance; indeed, "energy" and "method" were watchwords of both his politics and his life. A skilled wordsmith, he poured himself into his writings, defending the Constitution, the national government and his reputation with like fervor. In moments of crisis, though, Hamilton could push too hard, say too much and compromise too little. More than once, he favored military solutions to domestic crises in the hopes of quashing resistance to government authority. He responded similarly to attacks against his character, launching affairs of honor or doing battle in print. Discomfited by the rumblings of democracy and intolerant of opposition to his policies, he spent his life imposing order as he felt it should be.

Thus Hamilton's complicated and conflicted life. One of the nation's most powerful men by the age of 34, he was a political has-been a decade later, destroyed by his passions. Yet even his excesses served a purpose. In the confusion of the republic's founding, with no precise model to follow, Hamilton declared himself the man with the answers, proposing bold policies and challenging expectations. As polarizing as his politics were—and indeed, they divided the country—they triggered

UNCOMMONLY CANDID *Hamilton's willingness to speak his mind made him an effective if polarizing figure.*

a conversation about the nation's destiny. In the push and pull of devising a government, someone had to start things off and stake a claim. Hamilton was that man.

In a sense, Hamilton had been training for that moment for decades. Born poor and illegitimate in the West Indies and orphaned at a young age, he escaped from obscurity by displaying his talents. Impressed by the young man's writerly flair, some locals raised charitable funds to send him to the North American colonies for a proper education. Arriving in New York in 1772, as the Revolution was brewing, Hamilton was swept up in the furor, becoming an ardent pamphleteer, a soldier yearning to commit acts of derring-do and, ultimately, one of Commander in Chief George Washington's aides-de-camp.

Hamilton's quick wits and nimble writing made him invaluable at headquarters, but he wanted more. With little money, few connections and no family to fall back on, he was desperate to earn a name for himself on the battlefield, and he got his chance at Yorktown in 1781. But his relationship with Washington proved far more valuable. Working at the general's side in the crisis of war, Hamilton gained his trust and support, the all-important anchor of his political career.

But Hamilton didn't place all his bets on Washington. He wrote lengthy letters to men of influence, filled with advice for strengthening the government and salvaging its finances. Even before the war was over, Hamilton's core precepts were in place, and he wasn't shy about promoting them; he was one of the nation's first and most insistent nationalists. Hamilton's other wartime investment in his future was his marriage to Elizabeth Schuyler. The daughter of the wealthy Philip Schuyler of New York, she would be a vital source of stability for Hamilton throughout the rest of his life.

THE FEDERAL CONVENTION of 1787 must have seemed like a dream come true to Hamilton, who by then had been arguing for a stronger national government for nearly a decade. As one of New York's three delegates, he finally had the power to effect change. Or so he thought—his politically cautious New York colleagues consistently outvoted him. Still, he had his say in a grandstanding six-hour speech on June 18, proposing a plan of government so extreme in its centralized authority that it branded him a monarchist, a charge that he refuted to the end of his days. His work during the ratification debate was more fruitful; he invited James Madison and John Jay to join him in writing a series of newspaper essays defending the proposed Constitution. Although many of those essays were first drafts rushed to press, *The Federalist* became a key political text with the launching of the government, and it remains so today.

In September 1789, President Washington made Hamilton the nation's first secretary of the Treasury, starting Hamilton's peak years of power. Entrusted with bringing order to the nation's chaotic finances, he had bigger ambitions, taking full advantage of the unstructured new government to advance public policy. He envisioned a nation fueled by industry, with a strong national government directed by a strong executive and stabilized by the support of the rich and powerful. He promoted this vision with a financial plan that included the national assumption of state debts incurred during the Revolution, the establishment of a national bank and the encouragement of manufacturing. Faced with resistance to his bank proposal, Hamilton argued for a broad construction of the Constitution that profoundly shaped the nature of national governance from that time forward.

In an agrarian nation of loosely linked states that jealously guarded their independence and interests, Hamilton's policies were lightning rods of controversy. For a time, he gloried in the maelstrom, marshalling congressmen to fight on his side while slashing at opponents in the press. As Thomas Jefferson put it, he was "a host within himself." The end results were a national divide between Hamiltonian Federalists and Jeffersonian Republicans, and the rise of what we now call the first party system.

Hamilton the nationalist was a divisive politician. By 1795, he was also a tired one. With the nation's finances in order and his family's own finances suffering, he resigned from office and returned to New York to practice law. But even in private life, Hamilton was plagued by slanders and scandal. Freed from the confines of his government post and no longer reporting to Washington, he responded by running wild in print. Accused of speculating in government funds in 1796, he countered the charges by confessing to adultery in a shocking tell-all pamphlet that stunned friends and enemies alike.

GRATEFUL POSTERITY *His Trinity Churchyard gravestone pays tribute to Hamilton the patriot, the soldier, the statesman.*

> *Hamilton the nationalist was a divisive politician. By 1795, he was also a tired one. Even in private life, Hamilton was plagued by slanders and scandal. Freed from the confines of his government post, he responded by running wild in print.*

Four years later, Hamilton stumbled again. Still eager to steer national policy, he secretly advised members of President John Adams's cabinet for years. When Adams found out, he flew into a rage, forcing out Hamilton's supporters and denouncing him as a "Creole Bastard" leading a British faction. Hamilton responded with a 45-page pamphlet that savaged Adams's character. But his effort to replace Adams with a more pliable candidate in the pending election instead divided his party, throwing victory to the Republicans. Condemned as "radically deficient in discretion" by his fellow Federalists, Hamilton fell from power.

The talents and traits that had raised Hamilton to prominence—voracious ambition, compulsive self-expression, bold self-assertion—had destroyed him. The bitter fruits of his excesses were all too apparent in his final years. Not long after he retreated to his family and the Grange, his newly completed country home in the northern part of Manhattan, his private life was shattered. In 1801 his eldest son Philip died defending his father's much-maligned reputation in a duel. The traumatized Hamilton never fully recovered.

But his political principles never wavered, nor did his habit of saying more than he should. In 1804, when Aaron Burr ran for governor of New York, Hamilton plunged back into politics to oppose him; convinced that Burr was a power-hungry opportunist, Hamilton had long before declared it his "religious duty" to oppose his foe's career. Confronted by written evidence of Hamilton's invective, Burr initiated an affair of honor. During the course of negotiations, each man insulted the other, making a duel unavoidable. On July 11, in Weehawken, N.J., Burr's shot pierced Hamilton's liver and lodged in his spine. He died the next day.

The outpouring of grief at Hamilton's death attests to his legacy. Although his vision of America's future was one of many, its power—both to polarize and to energize—was undeniable, much like the man himself.

Joanne B. Freeman is a professor of history and American studies at Yale University, the editor of Alexander Hamilton: Writings *(Library of America, 2001) and the author of* Affairs of Honor: National Politics in the New Republic *(Yale, 2001). Her next book explores physical violence in the U.S. Congress in the decades leading up to the Civil War.*

THE LIFE AND TIMES OF ALEXANDER HAMILTON

■ BY COURTNEY MIFSUD

JAN. 11, 1755 (Or 1757—the record is unclear, although evidence leans to the former.) Alexander Hamilton is born out of wedlock to James Hamilton and Rachel Faucette Lavien on the island of Nevis in the British West Indies.

FEBRUARY 1755 A year into the French and Indian War, George Washington leads nearly 2,000 men into the Ohio Territory in an unsuccessful bid against the French.

SEPT. 1, 1764 The Currency Act is passed by the British Parliament, prohibiting colonies from issuing their own paper money and causing the destabilization of their economy.

MARCH 1765 Parliament passes the Stamp Act, which imposes the first direct tax on the colonies, and the Quartering Act, which forces colonists to house and feed British troops.

JULY 1765 The Sons of Liberty, a covert group of colonists that includes Samuel Adams and Benedict Arnold, forms in opposition to the Stamp Act.

FEB. 19, 1768 Rachel Faucette Lavien dies.

SEPT. 6, 1772 The *Royal Danish American Gazette* runs Hamilton's "Hurricane Letter," an eloquent description of the storm-wreaked destruction of St. Croix, his current island home. Impressed local dignitaries underwrite the teen's immigration to America to further his education.

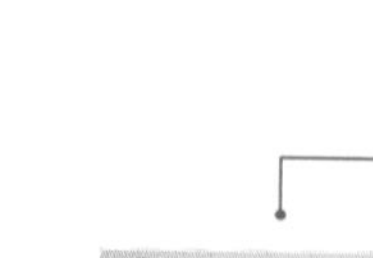

MAY 10, 1773 Parliament's Tea Act lowers the price of tea in the colonies but confirms their lack of representation in issues of taxation. The push for independence intensifies.

SUMMER 1773 Hamilton moves in with the William Livingston family in Elizabethtown, N.J., his first stateside residence. A few months later he is denied admission to the College of New Jersey (Princeton) and enrolls at King's College (Columbia, pictured above) in New York City instead.

DEC. 16, 1773 Colonial patriots dump 342 chests of tea into Boston Harbor to protest the Tea Act and, more generally, America's lack of representation in England's Parliament.

SEPT. 5, 1774 The first Continental Congress convenes in Philadelphia in response to the restrictive Intolerable Acts.

APRIL 18, 1775 Paul Revere sets off a-galloping to let Boston know the British are coming (specifically, for John Hancock and Samuel Adams).

1755 1755 1764 1765 1765 1768 1772 1773 1773 1773 1774 1775

1775 1775 1776 1776 1777 1780 1781 1781 1781 1781 1781 1782

APRIL 19, 1775 The Revolutionary War begins with clashes in the Massachusetts colony towns of Lexington and Concord.

JUNE 19, 1775 George Washington becomes commander in chief of the Continental Army.

MARCH 14, 1776 Shunning his studies, Hamilton enlists and receives a commission: artillery company captain.

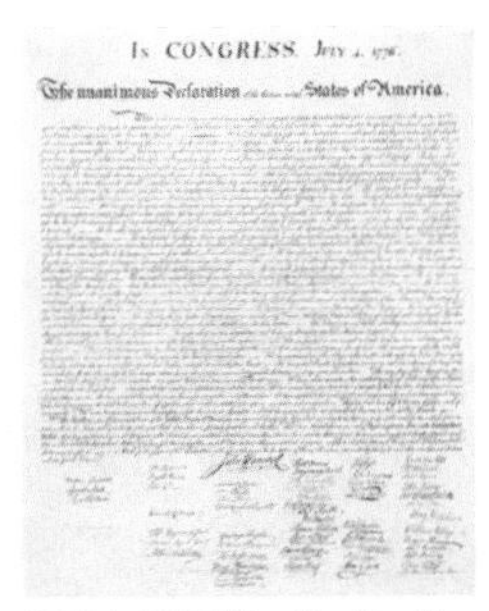
IN CONGRESS. July 4, 1776.

JULY 4, 1776 The Declaration of Independence is signed.

MARCH 1, 1777 Hamilton joins Washington as an aide-de-camp with the rank of lieutenant colonel.

DEC. 14, 1780 As the war rages, Hamilton finds time to wed Elizabeth Schuyler, the daughter of a wealthy and politically prominent family. They will have eight children together.

FEBRUARY 1781 Hamilton resigns his position with Washington; there are no hard feelings on either side.

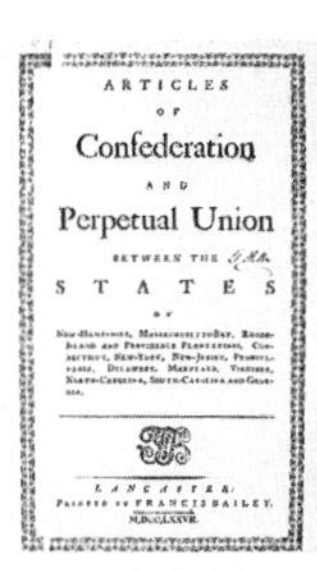
ARTICLES OF Confederation AND Perpetual Union BETWEEN THE STATES

LANCASTER: PRINTED BY FRANCIS BAILEY.

MARCH 1, 1781 The Articles of Confederation go into effect, uniting the sovereign states.

MAY 17, 1781 After being named the states' superintendent of finance, Robert Morris submits a plan for a national Bank of North America. Congress quickly approves.

JULY 1781 Washington awards Hamilton command of a light infantry battalion in the Marquis de Lafayette's corps.

OCT. 14, 1781 With only a bayonet, Hamilton subdues a British officer in Yorktown, Va. His heroics are heralded throughout the nation.

JULY 1782 Hamilton is admitted to the New York state bar—before fulfilling a required three-year law office training period.

(Continued on next page)

THE LIFE AND TIMES OF ALEXANDER HAMILTON

(continued from preceding page)

OCT. 25, 1782 Hamilton is named a New York delegate to the Continental Congress.

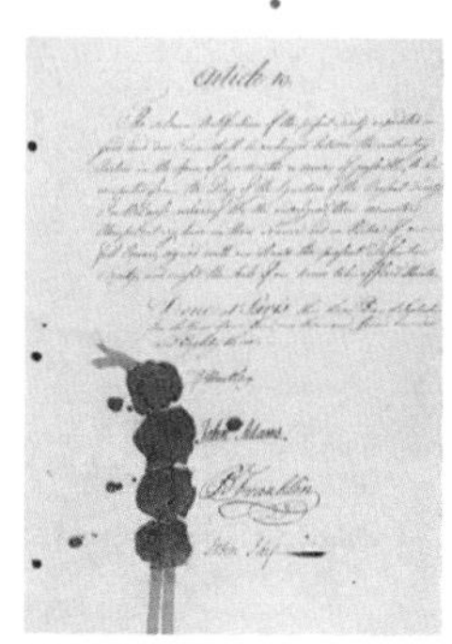

Article 10

John Adams.

B Franklin

SEPT. 3, 1783
The Treaty of Paris is signed, officially ending the Revolutionary War.

SEPT. 14, 1786 At a regional meeting in Annapolis, Md., Hamilton proposes a federal convention to revise the Articles of Confederation. The motion passes.

JULY 13, 1787 The Northwest Ordinance is adopted, installing the process by which states can enter the union.

We the People

SEPT. 17, 1787 The U.S. Constitution is signed, capping off a four-month convention in Philadelphia to create the document, and with it comes a new and enduring governmental framework.

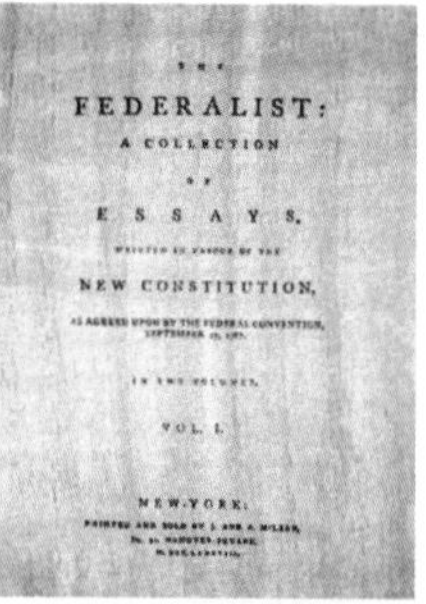
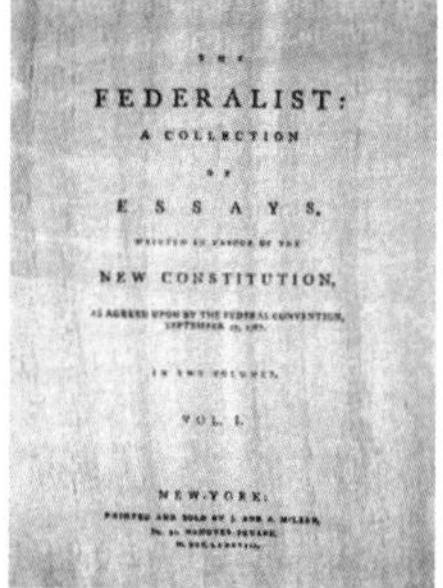

THE FEDERALIST:
A COLLECTION
OF
ESSAYS,
WRITTEN IN FAVOUR OF THE
NEW CONSTITUTION,
IN TWO VOLUMES.
VOL. I.
NEW-YORK:

MAY 28, 1788 The bound edition of *The Federalist Papers*, written to defend the proposed Constitution, is published; 51 of the 85 essays contained within are authored by Hamilton.

APRIL 30, 1789 Washington takes the oath of office as the unanimously elected first president of the United States.

SEPT. 11, 1789 Hamilton is appointed the first U.S. secretary of the Treasury.

REPORT
OF THE
SECRETARY of the TREASURY
TO THE
HOUSE of REPRESENTATIVES,
RELATIVE TO A PROVISION
FOR THE
SUPPORT
OF THE
PUBLIC CREDIT
OF THE
UNITED STATES.

JAN. 14, 1790 In the first of two "Reports on the Public Credit," Hamilton proposes that the federal government fund the national debt and assume the debt of each state as well.

DEC. 14, 1790 Hamilton presents a third paper, "Report on a National Bank," to urge the creation of a Bank of the United States. Wielding more power than the existing Bank of North America, it would issue paper money and act as the government's fiscal agent.

FEB. 25, 1791 Washington signs off on Hamilton's national-bank plan.

OBSERVATIONS
ON
CERTAIN DOCUMENTS
CONTAINED IN NO. V & VI OF
"THE HISTORY OF THE UNITED STATES
FOR THE YEAR 1796,"
IN WHICH THE
CHARGE OF SPECULATION
AGAINST
ALEXANDER HAMILTON,
LATE SECRETARY OF THE TREASURY,
IS FULLY REFUTED.
WRITTEN BY HIMSELF.
PHILADELPHIA:

SUMMER 1791 When an affair with Maria Reynolds comes to light amid accusations of blackmail, Hamilton releases a 95-page tell-all pamphlet to get ahead of what becomes America's first sex scandal.

1782 | 1783 | 1786 | 1787 | 1787 | 1788 | 1789 | 1789 | 1790 | 1790 | 1791 | 1791

DEC. 5, 1791 Hamilton submits his "Report on Manufactures," in which he proposes laws designed to aid the growth of industry by breaking Britain's hold on American trade.

JAN. 31, 1795 Hamilton retires as Treasury secretary and resumes the practice of law.

JULY 18, 1798 Over President John Adams's opposition, Washington appoints Hamilton as the country's inspector general, second in command of the U.S. Army. (As the army's commander in chief, Washington could determine his own chain of command.)

FEB. 18, 1799 With France upset at America's neutrality in the European wars, President Adams sends a peace mission overseas; tensions ease in what becomes known as the XYZ Affair.

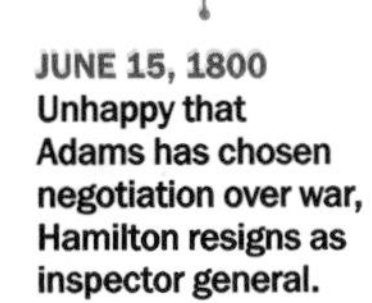

JUNE 15, 1800 Unhappy that Adams has chosen negotiation over war, Hamilton resigns as inspector general.

FEB. 11, 1801 Presidential candidates Thomas Jefferson and Aaron Burr deadlock in the Electoral College. Delaware's representative breaks the impasse, tipping the vote in Jefferson's favor.

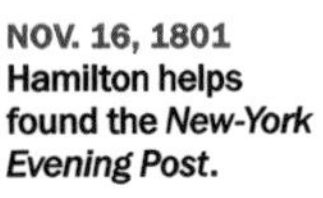

NOV. 16, 1801 Hamilton helps found the *New-York Evening Post*.

NOV. 22, 1801 Philip, Hamilton's eldest son, is mortally wounded while defending his father's honor in a duel with George I. Eacker. The lawyer had suggested that Hamilton favored monarchy over democracy.

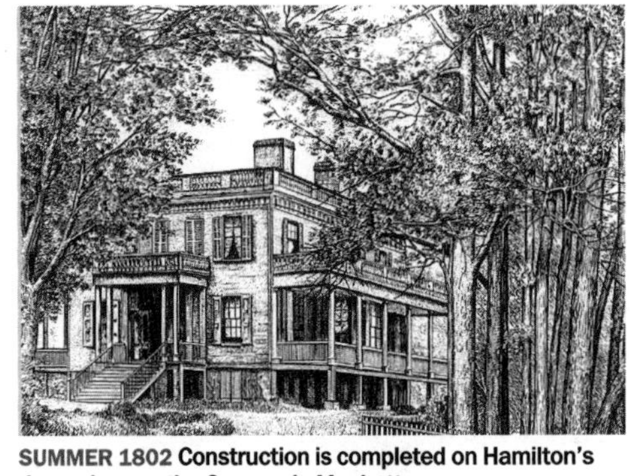

SUMMER 1802 Construction is completed on Hamilton's dream house: the Grange, in Manhattan.

APRIL 30, 1803 The Louisiana Purchase Treaty is signed by Envoy Extraordinary James Monroe and Robert Livingston in Paris.

JULY 11, 1804 Hamilton duels at dawn with Burr in Weehawken, N.J., months after Hamilton's most recent degrading opinions draw the attention of his longtime political and personal rival.

JULY 12, 1804 Hamilton dies in New York City. He is laid to rest at Trinity Church two days later.

1791 | 1795 | 1798 | 1799 | 1800 | 1801 | 1801 | 1801 | 1802 | 1803 | 1804 | 1804

TROUBLE IN PARADISE: A FOUNDING FATHER'S ISLAND YOUTH

How does an illegitimate son born to a ne'er-do-well father on a tiny Caribbean island become an American icon? It takes an act of God

BY DANIEL S. LEVY

THE CARIBBEAN ISLAND OF NEVIS isn't the first place you'd think to look for one of America's Founding Fathers. This northern member of the Leeward Islands chain is just an oval speck, the vestige of the volcanic peak at its center. Towering waterfalls, lush deep gorges and hot sulfur springs mark Nevis as a tropical paradise. Its dense rain forests swarm with Antillean crested hummingbirds and Pallas's mastiff bats—not to mention the descendants of the African Vervet monkeys brought ashore by the French in the 17th century. The turquoise waters that lap against its coarse sandy beaches are home to spiny lobsters, green turtles and spinner dolphins.

Yet it was on Nevis, in the harbor town of Charlestown, that Alexander Hamilton—future aide-de-camp to Gen. George Washington, author of *The Federalist Papers*, signer of the U.S. Constitution and steward of the nascent American economy—was born. And it was on Nevis and the neighboring island of St. Croix that Hamilton endured the harsh childhood that steeled him for the high-stakes battles that awaited him as an adult.

Hamilton's mother, Rachel Faucette, was born on Nevis around 1729. Her parents, John and Mary, owned a plantation on which they raised sugar, the "white gold" that made that part of the world so prosperous. By the 18th century, the island was attracting a melting pot

BEYOND THE HORIZON *As an illegitimate child growing up in the Caribbean (Pinney's Beach, Nevis, in the foreground, with St. Kitts in the distance), Hamilton could only dream of a larger life.*

of treasure seekers. John was French Huguenot and Mary was British, but Nevis also welcomed an assortment of Irish, Jewish and Spanish residents. Not all of them were wealthy planters and merchants. The sugar colonies were also a human dumping ground for the British, a place to exile, as one islander put it, "whole Ship-loads of her own Filth and Vermin, such as white Pick-pockets, Whores, Rogues, Vagrants, Thieves, &c. whom she judges not bad enough for the Gallows, and yet too bad to live among their virtuous Countrymen in England."

OF COURSE, THE CASH-CROP society could not have thrived if not on the backs of slaves. Ships packed with shackled Africans alit in Charlestown harbor. Before long, the island's 1,000 whites were outnumbered 4 to 1, then 8 to 1, by its blacks. Nevis was a rigidly stratified society, but the diseases that periodically ravaged the community—yellow fever, malaria, dysentery—were class- and race-blind. Five of Rachel's six siblings died young. So after her father breathed his last in 1745, she inherited what her famous son would one day call a "snug fortune." After burying her father, she took it and her mother 140 miles west to Christiansted on St. Croix.

Wherever she landed, the smart and pretty 16-year-old was going to be a valuable catch. Unfortunately, the eye she caught belonged to Johann Michael Lavien, a ne'er-do-well 30-year-old Dane, who saw a wife with an inheritance as the shortcut to his dream of becoming a successful planter. As Hamilton later described the unsavory courtship, "a fortune-hunter . . . came to Nevis bedizzened with gold, and paid his addresses to my mother then a handsome young woman." The couple settled on Lavien's plantation, Contentment—but despite the name, the union yielded other emotions entirely. Rachel had a child, Peter, but Lavien was an inept businessman and squandered his wife's money. It was, as Hamilton later described it, "a hated marriage."

Which she left, none too soon, around 1750. Enraged by the affront, Lavien set off a chain of events that would forever taint her and her unborn children. Danish law at the time gave a husband the right to imprison an adulterous, deserting wife. Lavien trumped up charges of infidelity that landed Rachel behind bars inside the town fort. She spent the next hellish months in a small cell, surviving on salted herring, cornmeal mush and cod. In the end, however, the experience didn't break her, and upon her release, Rachel sailed with her mother to the island of St. Kitts.

On first impression, James Hamilton presented as the opposite of Johann Lavien. Hamilton was well born, the fourth of 11 children of a father, Alexander, who was a laird of Grange in the county of Ayshire in southwestern Scotland. James left the family castle in 1741 to seek his fortune across the ocean. Lacking both business sense and industriousness, though, Hamilton was struggling by the time he met Rachel on St. Kitts. Still, he charmed the young woman in need of a fresh start. Soon the pair had entered into a common-law marriage, addressed as Mr. and Mrs. James Hamilton even though it was well known that Rachel was another man's wife. James Jr. arrived in 1753. By the time Alexander was born, on Jan. 11, 1755, the family had relocated to Nevis.

The wooden buildings and narrow streets of Charlestown bustled with merchants and traders, pirates and old salts. From his home, the young Alexander, remembered by a mentor as "rather delicate & frail," could hear the buzz of the docks as cargo was unloaded and deals were struck. But he did not feel welcome there. His parents' unofficial union meant that the handsome boy with the red hair and piercing violet eyes was viewed as a bastard child. The illegitimacy racked Hamilton throughout his life. "My birth is the subject of the most humiliating criticism," he reluctantly admitted in future years. Being "not free from blemish," Hamilton was likely not allowed to attend an Anglican school. In any case, he studied with a tutor.

In 1759, when Hamilton was 4, Lavien, looking to remarry, began divorce proceedings. He

> *Unfortunately, the eye she caught belonged to Johann Michael Lavien, who saw a wife with an inheritance as the shortcut to his dream of becoming a successful planter.*

LONG WAY TO GO *The first secretary of the Treasury was born in this home on Nevis in 1755.*

WHITE GOLD MINE *Plantation owners throughout the sugar colonies built their fabulous fortunes on the backs of the African slaves who were shipped to the Caribbean islands by the thousands.*

defamed Rachel again, accusing her of "whoring with everyone" and having "completely forgotten her duty" by abandoning her one legitimate child. For good measure, he also referred to the younger Hamiltons as "whore-children." Lavien got his divorce, and in the process the court also denied Rachel the right to remarry.

A few years later, James landed a job as head clerk for a tobacco merchant on St. Croix, and he moved the family to Christiansted. Soon after, though, he abandoned his wife and sons. Surprisingly, Alexander later defended the neglectful move in a letter to an uncle in Scotland: "You no doubt have understood that my fathers affairs at a very early day went to wreck; so as to have rendered his situation during the greatest part of his life far from eligible." Alexander never saw his father again, and he received no response after inviting the man to his wedding in 1780.

RACHEL WAS LEFT TO RAISE her boys alone in a community well aware of her reputation, however unfairly it was gained. Christiansted was not a large city; everyone's social station was plainly evident for others to see. There was wealth: rich children rode to dancing schools in ornate carriages. And there was tawdriness: a string of brothels and taverns lined the town's dark alleys. But there was also commingling of the races: groups of multiethnic children played in the streets. Hamilton would later be incorrectly identified by political enemies as a quarter, or even an eighth, black.

Rachel did her best, but, abandoned and scorned, she inevitably found herself in need of

SPLIT IMAGE *There are two young Hamiltons: the boy who was buffeted by questions of his childhood on Nevis (above, in a stereoscopic view of his birthplace) and the brash teenager who quickly reinvented himself as an American in Manhattan.*

some help. She received it from her brother-in-law, James Lytton, who paid the rent on their two-story house. Rachel and the boys lived on the second floor. They kept a goat in the yard, and Alexander, an avid reader, shelved his books in their rooms. Rachel ran a general store out of the first floor, where she sold beef, salted fish, flour, rice and other supplies that she bought from her landlord and from two New York merchants, David Beekman and Nicholas Cruger, who ran a trading firm on the island. Rachel owned five female slaves and their children, and she rented them out when she was short of money. The Hamiltons weren't exactly the privileged class, but they were making their way.

Then in early 1768, both Alexander and Rachel came down with a virulent fever. Sharing a sick bed, they endured the barbaric treatments of the era together. One doctor bled Alexander to rebalance his body's "humors." Rachel was prescribed medicine to make her vomit and an herbal "remedy" with laxative properties. Mother and son, withering from these useless ministrations, lay side by side in their own excretions. Alexander recovered. Rachel did not. She died on February 19.

Because she was a divorced woman, the church likely denied her a proper funeral, which may be why she was laid to rest on her sister's estate. Making matters worse for her essentially orphaned children, Lavien reappeared, insisting that Peter, the son he had with Rachel, was her sole heir. Rachel didn't have much, but what she did own, Lavien argued successfully, was now his. Alexander and James, condemned again as children of "whoredom," were successfully disinherited.

The impoverished Hamilton boys were taken in by their cousin, Peter Lytton, but in quick succession he committed suicide and his father, the boys' onetime benefactor James, died too. The 14-year-old Alexander had recently begun to clerk for those New York suppliers, Beekman and Cruger. (His brother was working as a carpenter's apprentice.) Now he was taken in by another local merchant, Thomas Stevens, and his wife. One of the couple's five children, Edward, became Hamilton's closest friend. In fact, the two shared an uncanny resemblance that led many to surmise that the elder Stevens was Hamilton's actual father—a fact that, if true, would explain why he had so readily welcomed the young teen into his home.

Though the vengeful Lavien had snatched away Rachel's few material possessions, Hamilton definitely came away with her smarts. And

> *Mother and son, withering from useless ministrations, lay side by side with virulent fevers. Alexander recovered. Rachel did not.*

COMING INTO FOCUS *This early portrait was created around the time Hamilton arrived in America.*

at last secure, ensconced in a proper new home and a challenging new job, he began to blossom. Exposed to the worlds of economics, trade and politics, Hamilton was transformed. He learned to write clearly and balance books. He polished his French and handled foreign currencies: British pounds, Dutch stivers, Spanish pieces of eight and Danish ducats. He sorted through inventories, negotiated with crusty ship captains and cracked the secrets of traders and smugglers alike. Later, Hamilton would refer to his time at the merchants' house as "the most useful of his education."

The exporter-importers owned a shop and a warehouse in town as well as a dock and a ship. Their firm served the needs of local planters: flour, rice, timber, beer, beef, cider, mules and cattle. It also dealt in slaves, transporting hundreds to the islands. Hamilton had to appraise the new arrivals. This was one part of the job he most assuredly did not enjoy, and he opposed slavery when he got the chance, later in America.

PAID LEAVE *Hamilton's journey north was underwritten by local merchants like Nicholas Cruger.*

As he became acquainted with the larger world beyond the Lesser Antilles, Hamilton began to imagine greater adventures and glory for himself. In November 1769, he wrote to his friend Edward, who had headed off to King's College in New York, of his frustrations: "Ned, my Ambition is [so] prevalent that I contemn the grov'ling and condition of a Clerk or the like, to which my Fortune &c. condemns me and would willingly risk my life tho' not my Character to exalt my Station .... Im no Philosopher you see and may be jus[t]ly said to Build Castles in the Air.... I shall Conclude [by] saying I wish there was a War."

The unfulfilled romantic began to write poetry as an outlet for his longing, and the island's *Royal Danish American Gazette* published his precocious verse about love and religion. He also fell under the tutelage of the Rev. Hugh Knox, the minister of the local Scotch Presbyterian church and a part-time editor at the *Gazette*. Knox guided the bookish young man's education, offering him access to his library and influencing him with his liberal views, including an opposition to slavery. (Knox studied divinity at what is now Princeton University under Aaron Burr, the father of Hamilton's eventual assassin.) The 17-year-old may not have been satisfied by the life he had carved out for himself, but from the outside he looked very much like what he was: one of the town's up-and-coming merchant clerks.

Then, on Aug. 31, 1772, a devastating storm tore through the Caribbean. What the *Gazette* called the "most dreadful Hurricane known in the memory of man" raged unabated over St. Croix for six hours, destroying homes and refineries, ripping up trees, flattening cane fields and sweeping away boats. A simultaneous tidal wave, likely the result of an earthquake on Nevis, further pummeled the island. Once the sky cleared, Hamilton wrote a letter to his father to describe what happened. Before sending it, he showed it to Knox, who encouraged him to have it published.

HAMILTON'S RECOUNTING of the hurricane appeared in the *Gazette* on October 3. It read in part: "The roaring of the sea and wind, fiery meteors flying about it in the air, the prodigious glare of almost perpetual lightning, the crash of the falling houses, and the ear-piercing shrieks of the distressed, were sufficient to strike astonishment into Angels. A great part of the buildings throughout the Island are levelled to the ground, almost all the rest very much shattered; several persons killed and numbers utterly ruined; whole families running about the streets, unknowing where to find a place of shelter; the sick exposed to the keeness of water and air without a bed to lie upon, or a dry covering to their bodies; and our harbours entirely bare. In a word, misery, in all its most hideous shapes, spread over the whole face of the country." The published letter immediately revealed the erudition and ability of this uncanny youth to all on the island, from the governor on down. A collection was taken up to help send Hamilton to America, where he could get a proper education. Within months, he was boarding a boat and bidding good-bye to the only world he knew.

"The changes in the human conditions are uncertain and frequent," he would note 16 years later during a debate over the adoption of the U.S. Constitution. "Many, on whom fortune has bestowed her favours, may trace their family to a more unprosperous station; and many who are now in obscurity, may look back upon the affluence and exalted rank of their ancestors." But when he set sail that day, he could have no idea of what awaited him in the British colonies of North America. He knew only that he had been given a chance to challenge the presumed fate of a child born to a woman wrongly judged.

Fortunately, as his ship slipped from the harbor of St. Croix, he carried with him more than his few earthly belongings. He carried too the gifts bequeathed to him by his mother: an extraordinary drive and a Herculean will, both of which he would have to call upon again as he joined the fight to mold a new nation.

Lighting the Way for Sailors

As his storm-tossed brig passed North Carolina's Cape Hatteras on the way to New York in the early 1770s, a fearful Hamilton vowed to someday build a way-finding lighthouse there. In 1789, Congress passed An Act for the Establishment and support of Lighthouse, Beacons, Buoys, and Public Piers, and the job of maintaining those structures was given to the Department of the Treasury. Thus did Hamilton find himself the "Superintendent" of Lighthouses. His first commission, which rose near the entrance to the Chesapeake Bay, was designed by John McComb Jr., who would one day build the Grange, Hamilton's New York home. And in 1803 a promise was kept, as "Mr. Hamilton's Light" opened on Cape Hatteras.

SENTINEL *Hamilton's lighthouse at Cape Hatteras was rebuilt after the original succumbed to erosion.*

THE EDUCATION OF A REVOLUTIONARY

A precocious island boy came to America to get some proper schooling. But the life-changing lessons he ended up learning were not taught in any classroom

BY DANIEL S. LEVY

HAMILTON'S JOURNEY NORTH TO HIS new life was by no means smooth sailing: his ship caught fire at sea, and it took a day to douse the flames. After three hard weeks, the damaged brig slipped into Boston Harbor. Hamilton immediately headed south to see about entering the College of New Jersey. His previous education being haphazard at best, he knew he needed to prepare for the entrance exam, so he enrolled at the Elizabethtown Academy in Elizabethtown, N.J., to bone up on Virgil and Cicero, Latin and Greek. The extra work did the trick; he aced the test.

Yet the college—Princeton today—rejected St. Croix's prodigal son. According to a friend, Hercules Mulligan, the school was not in favor of Hamilton's intention to finish "with as much rapidity as his exertions would enable him to do." The rejection was a blow; at the time, the colonies were home to just eight other colleges. In the end, Hamilton didn't have to look far for a second choice. Back across the Hudson River stood King's College.

In the early 1770s, some 25,000 people lived on Manhattan Island, most on its developed southern end. The multilingual city on the harbor boasted a growing merchant class, a volatile political climate and combative newspapers. Here was a place where Hamilton would not only fit in but blossom.

He entered King's College in late 1773 or early 1774. The school, which after the revolution would be rechristened Columbia College, occupied a single building in a meadow overlooking the river. As one of its 17 students, Hamilton wore a cap and gown and studied the classics, geography, philosophy, math, science and rhetoric. He dove into the political philosophies of John Locke, Thomas Hobbes, David Hume, Montesquieu and others. But even as he crammed to make up for lost classroom time, he also took part in extracurricular literary societies and helped found a club in which students discussed politics and honed writing and public speaking skills. In that club, according to Robert Troup, Hamilton "made extraordinary displays of richness of genius and energy of mind."

King's College was Loyalist-run, a conservative institution with an Anglican minister, Myles Cooper, in charge. That too suited Hamilton—as a child of the Caribbean, he had already sworn al-

SAFETY SCHOOL *King's College stood, according to one visitor, on "the most beautiful site for a college in the world."*

legiance to the monarchy, so the school felt like a familiar home. But the fence that surrounded it was not nearly tall enough to keep out the intruder closing in. Down the road, on the grassy field that was the city's Common, a pole supported a gilded weather vane. At the top was the word LIBERTY.

Even before Hamilton arrived on the mainland, the colonists were agitating. They resented the restrictions on self-rule—not to mention the attendant taxes—imposed by Parliament in legislation like the Stamp Act, enacted in 1765, and the Townshend Acts of two years later. In January 1770, members of the colonial underground, known as the Sons of Liberty, scuffled with British troops in the Battle of Golden Hill, resulting in a number of injuries. Two months later, on March 5, a bloodier confrontation broke out. Protesting the Townshend Acts and urging a boycott, five colonists were killed in what would become known as the Boston Massacre.

Then on Dec. 16, 1773, Boston patriots dressed as Mohawk Indians and dumped £18,000 of tea in their harbor to protest a tax on the kitchen staple. Seduced by the unrest, Hamilton took a trip to Boston, and upon his return he wrote a piece for the *New-York Journal*, "Defence and Destruction of the Tea." Meanwhile, in retaliation for the turmoil, Parliament imposed the Coercive Acts (Intolerable Acts to the Americans), which among other penalties shuttered Boston's port and enforced military rule. Far from cowing the colonists, though, the new laws spurred a total embargo of British goods.

It was all an exciting distraction for a political-minded student. Throughout New York, patriots posted broadsides and handbills, circulated petitions and staged rallies. The Sons of Liberty held one such event on the Common on July 6, 1774. The quickly radicalizing Hamilton stepped up to voice support for the Tea Party and the boycott, predicting that they would "prove the salvation of

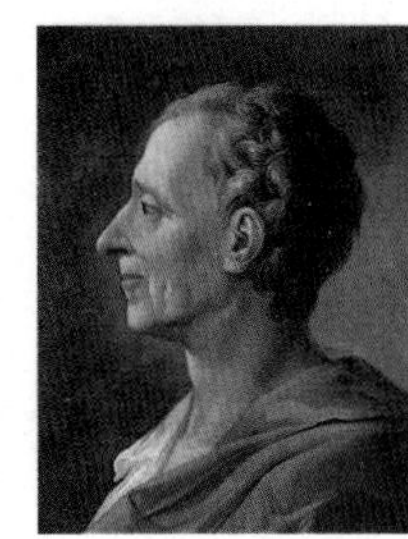

WRITERS' BLOC *Hamilton read voraciously the works of, from far left, John Locke, Thomas Hobbes, David Hume and Charles-Louis de Montesquieu.*

North America and her liberties." His mature oration elicited enthusiastic applause amid surprised observations of his being but a "collegian."

Not everyone, however, embraced the defiance. At King's College, President Cooper smeared the Sons of Liberty as "sons of licentiousness." And the Loyalist Rev. Samuel Seabury branded the members of the summer's First Continental Congress "a venomous brood of scorpions." Hamilton could not let Seabury's slanderous writing pass. His 35-page rebuttal, *A Full Vindication of the Measures of the Congress*, revealed its 19-year-old author to have an uncanny knowledge of politics, British law, history and philosophy. When Seabury responded, Hamilton penned the even longer *The Farmer Refuted*, which featured what would become his trademark one-two punch: slashing accusation and glib articulation of issues. Hamilton called the minister's charges "puerile and fallacious" and argued that the colonists had the "power to . . . harass and exhaust the soldiery" until there was a peace.

Soon after, war broke out. On April 19, 1775, British Redcoats, on their way to seize the colonists' military stores in Concord, Mass., passed through nearby Lexington. There, they were met by 77 colonial militiamen—Minutemen—and other volunteers on the local green. Shots were exchanged, and the colonists retreated. Later, "the shot heard round the world" was fired at Concord as a few hundred Americans attacked the British.

Once word of the open rebellion trickled south, New Yorkers "paraded the town with drums beating and colours flying," wrote Judge Thomas Jones. The Sons of Liberty seized 1,000 weapons from the City Hall arsenal. Militias sprang up, and Hamilton joined one, the Hearts of Oak (alternatively known as the Corsicans). But even as he brimmed with revolutionary fervor and read up on military tactics, he could not shake his aversion to mob action. On May 10, hundreds of townspeople descended on King's College, intent on tarring and feathering its Loyalist president. According to Troup, Hamilton "instantly resolved to take his stand on the stairs in front of the Doctor's apartment." Berating the crowd, he detained it long enough for Cooper to climb the school's fence and flee.

ENEMY OF THE PEOPLE *Hamilton could not let pass the Rev. Samuel Seabury's negative views on the uprising.*

THAT MONTH, THE H.M.S. *Asia*, a British 64-gun man-of-war, sailed into New York Harbor. Within weeks, the Second Continental Congress met in the Pennsylvania State House (better known today as Independence Hall) to appoint Col. George Washington head of the Continental Army. And on June 17, 1775, the Revolution's first real combat—the Battle of Bunker Hill, though it unfolded on Breed's Hill—transpired. By August, King George III was forced to recognize that his colonies had "at length proceeded to open and avowed rebellion."

With the *Asia* anchored offshore, the patriots feared that the British might try to seize the cannons at Fort George, on Manhattan's southern tip. So on the same day that the king castigated the upstart colonists, Hamilton and 15 of his classmates set out to move the weaponry to safety. "I recollect well that Mr. Hamilton was there," wrote Hercules Mulligan, "for I was engaged in hauling off one of the cannon when Mr. H. came up and gave me his musket to hold and he took hold of the rope." As they carried out the mission, soldiers on a barge launched from the *Asia* shot at them. When Hamilton and the others returned fire, the warship shot off a barrage of cannonballs and grapeshot. The revolutionaries got away—unscathed—with the cannons, and dragged them uptown to the Common.

Between late 1775 and the start of 1776, Hamilton wrote a series of pieces about the growing tensions for the *New-York Journal*. Meanwhile, a little-known immigrant from Thetford, England, printed a 50-page pamphlet, *Common Sense*, that mocked monarchy. "One of the strongest natural proofs of the folly of hereditary right in kings, is that nature disapproves it, otherwise, she would not so frequently turn it into ridicule by giving mankind an *Ass for a Lion*," Thomas Paine wrote.

LIBERTY OR DEATH *Minutemen first confronted the British on the Lexington Green on April 19, 1775.*

His appeal for independence quickly sold 500,000 copies and galvanized Americans.

Those Americans continued to terrorize New York's remaining Loyalists. Hamilton, now 21, put the finishing touches on the 14th of his *Journal* essays, then joined the Continental Army. With his transformation to soldier complete, he wanted to make sure that those living in his old homeland understood the depth of his commitment: "I was born to die and my reason and conscience tell me it is impossible to die in a better or more important cause," he wrote in one of his regular reports to St. Croix's newspaper, the *Royal Danish American Gazette*.

With New York under siege, the rebels closed off streets, threw up defensive batteries and shut down King's College. In March 1776 the government commissioned Hamilton a captain in the army and charged him with raising an artillery company. Among his duties was overseeing the construction of a fort just northeast of the Common. In June, Capt. Hamilton led 100 men against a British-controlled lighthouse at Sandy Hook, on the coast of New Jersey. Unfortunately, the enemy were ready for them. Hamilton regretted that his men "could make no impression on the walls."

> *"I was born to die and my reason and conscience tell me it is impossible to die in a better or more important cause."*
>
> —ALEXANDER HAMILTON, IN ST. CROIX'S *ROYAL DANISH AMERICAN GAZETTE*

The shadow of full British might finally darkened the horizon on June 29. As rifleman Daniel McCurtin looked out over New York Harbor, he was stunned to see 110 ships transporting 9,000 troops led by Gen. William Howe and Adm. Richard Howe: "I declare that I thought all London was afloat." With some 20,000 soldiers under his command, Washington bemoaned his position. Recognizing that they were "extremely deficient in arms," he had them melt down roof and window lead for bullets. Days later, on July 4, the Continental Congress announced "The unanimous Declaration of the thirteen united States of America."

Four years earlier, a hurricane had swept Hamilton off St. Croix. Now another storm was gathering force off the coast of his new home, soon to make landfall. Hamilton had always dreamed of waging war. That dream was about to come true.

A VICTOR'S SPOILS

What is war good for? Making a reputation and igniting an illustrious career

BY LILY ROTHMAN

HAMILTON'S MILITARY CAREER BEGAN with a bang—and not in a good way. About a week after the adoption of the Declaration of Independence, the young captain got his chance to pit his artillery company against two British ships. It would be his first foray into battle leadership. But one of the company cannons exploded, killing or wounding several of the men, and the ships escaped unharmed.

The mishap did not dull Hamilton's eagerness for action. For about a year, he had juggled academic studies with military training. In fact, his determination to learn on his own the tactical and practical skills needed to wage war was the reason he'd been recommended for an officer's position in the first place. With the need to fight growing more urgent, he had quit his schoolwork to focus full time on the task at hand. War burnished reputations, and he was consumed with his own. But though he might have wished otherwise, the glory of his martial successes would pale before less bloody—but equally crucial—duties.

The British attack on New York was a depressing beginning for the new nation. The city, already a hub of New World financial activity, fell by mid-September. Backed by Hessian forces—German mercenaries—the redcoats easily advanced through Brooklyn and into Manhattan. Though Gen. George Washington and his troops were forced to retreat to New Jersey, Hamilton's bravery impressed his commander.

Come Christmas, Washington commanded one of the most famous maneuvers of the war: the crossing of the icy Delaware River to attack the Hessians camped in Trenton, N.J. Hamilton was one of the officers responsible for directing the cannon fire that was doubly important because it both prevented the enemy from forming ranks (clearing the way for the American infantry) and blocked their escape routes. The well-conceived victory was an important psychological turning point, arriving as it did after a long run of losses. Hamilton's steady performance at Trenton—even more noteworthy because he was ill for much of that winter—and at another battle in nearby Princeton marked him for a quick rise through the ranks.

That rise occurred soon enough, if likely not the way the eager-for-the-fight Hamilton imag-

READY FOR ACTION *As an artillery officer during the Revolution, Hamilton was eager to be a leader in the colonists' quest for freedom—and to burnish his reputation.*

ALLIANCE *Gen. Washington developed a great deal of respect for his officer Hamilton, who rapidly ascended the ranks to become his aide-de-camp.*

ined it would. Within weeks, he was summoned to army headquarters; Washington wanted him to join his staff. In March 1777, Hamilton wrote to the Convention of the Representatives of the State of New-York to advise them that "His Excellency has been pleased to appoint me one of his Aid du Camps" and that they would have to find someone else to lead his company.

Still, Hamilton had mixed feelings about accepting. Being the general's right-hand man would significantly raise the social cachet of a man who'd had to build his from scratch. But he remained tempted by the respect that could be won only in the field. "He was conscious of staff officers not making it into the history books," says Philip Mead, a curator at the Museum of the American Revolution (which opens in 2017 in Philadelphia).

Nonetheless, it was as Washington's trusted assistant that Hamilton spent much of the rest of the war. And it was from that position that he embarked on the path that would assure his place in history. "We tend to look for field commands and battle valor when we're talking about military contributions," Mead says, "but when Washington and his aides were trying to create a functioning national army, they were accomplishing an extraordinary task in that they were also creating the first American national institution of any real size."

Hamilton was instrumental in the success of that task, with contributions that ranged from crafting new rules for the troops—for example, barring off-duty detachments from undressing at night when the enemy was nearby—to drafting correspondence to French allies. (His French Huguenot mother had taught him the language back in the Caribbean.) Though he continued to seek opportunities to fight, it was from behind a desk that Hamilton shone.

Linked so closely to Washington, Hamilton also got the chance to meet the well-positioned men who would become confidants, not to mention his future wife, Elizabeth Schuyler. Born of a prominent New York family, she would have been otherwise out of reach.

The fatherless Hamilton may have seen his general as more than a boss, especially as Washington referred to his staff as family—at least until an unremarkable morning in February 1781, when the two had a strange encounter. Passing Hamilton, now a lieutenant colonel, on the stairs, Washington asked for his attention; Hamilton responded with the 18th-century equivalent of "be there in a second" and then continued on his errand, which he described later in a letter to his father-in-law as urgent. On his way back to Washington, he ran into the Marquis de Lafayette, who waylaid him with an issue of his own. By the time Hamilton returned, his commander was not pleased. " 'Col Hamilton,' Washington said, 'you have kept me waiting at the head of the stairs these ten minutes,' " the younger man reported in the letter, before adding that the minutes passed were more like two. So when Washington said he felt disrespected, Hamilton responded—respectfully—that if Washington was serious, then that was that; Hamilton could not work for a man who thought him capable of such a dishonorable act. "I am no longer a member of the General's family," his letter declared.

Some suspect Hamilton had been waiting for an excuse to quit. To his father-in-law he acknowledged disliking his position of "personal dependence," even to a man he so admired. Plus, leaving Washington's staff could mean the possibility of returning to the battlefield. Of course, Hamilton could well have thought the scolding left him no choice. Aspersions on his character were no small matter.

Following the confrontation, Hamilton quickly put aside any potential awkwardness and began to lobby for a battlefield assignment. In petitioning Washington directly, he pointed out that had he never joined the General's staff, he "ought in justice to have been more advanced in rank than I now am." That July, Washington put Hamilton in charge of a light-infantry battalion from New York.

THE COMMISSION CAME JUST in time. The war's momentum had turned. France was fighting on America's side, and the progress of the British on most northerly fronts was stalled. A concentrated effort in the south was proving largely futile as well. Within a day of Hamilton's receiving his command, Britain's Gen. Charles Cornwallis led his troops to Yorktown, Va., a town on the deep harbor carved by the York River. The decision was a fateful one. Cornwallis counted on support from the sea, but his British ships were headed off by the French before they reached Chesapeake Bay. In the meantime, while decoying the British into thinking New York was the target, Washington's troops and their French allies made their way toward Yorktown. As the summer waned, the British found themselves surrounded by about twice as many Continental soldiers. Hamilton was among them.

The siege of Yorktown commenced at the end of September. The British had encircled their position with defensive shelters, but human reinforcements were far away. The Revolutionary army began to dig siege lines that allowed soldiers to move cannons closer and closer to Cornwallis's troops. On October 12, Hamilton wrote to his wife, "Thank heaven, our affairs seem to be approaching fast to a happy period." He figured that within five days the British would surrender or flee; if they did the latter, he predicted 10 more days to finish them off.

Hamilton's analysis was right on. He appealed to Washington again, this time to lead an attack on one of the fortifications standing in the way of victory. On October 14, Hamilton and his men rushed the position closest to the water. Clambering over the walls, they found themselves face to face with the British. Within minutes, the structure was theirs. Soon after, the other fortifications fell too.

Cornwallis surrendered on October 19. America's decisive victory at Yorktown announced that the American army had become a force to fear. As Hamilton wrote to his friend Lafayette, the "rapidity and immediate success of the assault are the best comment on the behaviour of the troops."

A treaty would not be signed until 1783, but the war was essentially over. And though it wasn't his last action—he helped President Washington end the anti-tax Whiskey Rebellion in 1794, for example—Hamilton's career as a soldier was essentially over too. He had accomplished all he meant to and more, with spoils that included a commander's respect, access to the most powerful people in the land, a wife—and, not least, a new country to call his own.

TURNING POINT *The surrender of British general Lord Cornwallis at Yorktown on Oct. 19, 1781, represented a major military triumph for the upstart Americans on their path to independence and a new nation.*

"WE CANNOT FAIL TO ALWAYS BE HAPPY"

Being married to an important man can be complicated. Alexander and Elizabeth Hamilton figured out how to make it work

BY SARAH BEGLEY

FEW MARRIAGES HAVE BEEN SO WARM YET so blighted as the union of Alexander Hamilton and Elizabeth Schuyler. Their two decades together withstood wartime turbulence, the births of eight children, the first sex scandal in the U.S. and the tragic loss of a firstborn son. Through it all, they regarded each other as soulmates.

As a young lieutenant colonel, Hamilton was known as a ladies' man. It was a reputation fairly earned. He made several romantic attachments to society women he met because of his military position; in one of the many amorous notes sent to one sweetheart, Kitty Livingston, he wrote, "ALL FOR LOVE is my motto."

But he eventually settled on the daughter of a wealthy general, Philip Schuyler. Hamilton met the woman known to him as Eliza or Betsey while on a mission for Gen. George Washington in Albany, N.Y., in 1777, but they became better acquainted two years later at Washington's winter headquarters in Morristown, N.J. The 25-year-old Hamilton was taken not only with Schuyler, who was 22, but her family as well, especially her sister Angelica. The fascination went both ways, as the two conducted an extremely affectionate correspondence until his death. But Angelica was married, so it was to Eliza that he professed his love. Writing to another Schuyler sister during the courtship, Hamilton said he thought Eliza "most unmercifully handsome" with "good nature, affability, and vivacity." She was in fact considered a great beauty. She was also tougher than many of her peers, making her worthy of the challenges she would face as Mrs. Hamilton.

The couple were married on Dec. 14, 1780, in a small ceremony at the Schuyler mansion. Hamilton, having taken leave from the war for the occasion, returned to service the next month. Eliza soon joined him at headquarters, which were now in New Windsor, N.Y. There, she became close with Martha Washington, who in her estimation was the pinnacle of womanhood.

Though Hamilton's religious zeal ebbed and flowed, Eliza was a devout member of the Dutch Reformed Church, and she trusted her husband's faith. She may not have been the intellect he was, but she was better connected—Benjamin Franklin, for one, taught her how to play backgammon—and she was well versed in the issues of the day.

ALEXANDER'S ANGEL *The portraitist Ralph Earl painted Elizabeth Hamilton in 1787, highlighting her striking dark eyes.*

For the first years of their marriage, Hamilton remained engaged in his military duties. Eliza was pregnant with their first child during the Battle of Yorktown, one of her husband's battlefield triumphs, and he wrote to ask that she deliver him a boy. He got his wish: Philip Schuyler Hamilton was born several months later.

Marrying into a prominent New York family helped Hamilton's postwar advancement—as a lawyer, Treasury secretary and inspector general of the army. Then again, marrying an up-and-comer had similar perks for Eliza. When Washington was sworn in, she attended the inaugural ball and danced with the man himself. She also hosted a dinner for Thomas Jefferson upon his return from his time as minister to France. (The Hamiltons may have lived to regret their hospitality, given the future rivalry between the two men.) And Eliza was invited to exclusive society events, enjoying them more than her friend Martha Washington did.

Eliza remained humble, though. She seems to have destroyed her own letters while carefully maintaining her husband's. That correspondence speaks only of marital bliss. Hamilton called his wife "charmer" and "angel," and when they were apart, he was anxious to reunite. "Happy, however, I cannot be, absent from you and my darling little ones," he wrote in 1786 after the birth of their third child. "I feel that nothing can ever compensate for the loss of the enjoyments I leave at home . . . Think of me with as much tenderness as I do of you and we cannot fail to be always happy."

FAMILY MATTERS *Eliza's sister Angelica, though married to John Barker Church, continued to correspond with Hamilton throughout his life.*

Hamilton was a doting father, balancing parental duties with his demanding career: when his work took him away from Eliza, he often took a couple of the older children with him. With eight kids in 20 years, plus a constant stream of orphans passing through the house, there was little respite. But children adored Hamilton, and men were sometimes surprised at how affectionate he was in return. Such a happy household made his decision to enter a vulgar affair all the more surprising.

In the summer of 1791, a woman went to Hamilton's home in Philadelphia, telling a story of an abusive husband who had run off, leaving her destitute. Hamilton agreed to bring money to her house. When he arrived, he later wrote, "Some conversation ensued from which it was quickly apparent that other than pecuniary consolation would be acceptable."

So began what may well be America's first political sex scandal. Hamilton's attachment to Maria (pronounced "Mariah") Reynolds lasted at least a year, even after her husband, James, began blackmailing Hamilton—$1,000 in exchange for his silence. Hamilton began to pay in installments, and he tried more than once to end the relationship, but each time either Maria or James would claim she was grief-stricken and he had to see her again. The entreaties have raised the question of whether the affair was devised as a trap from the start. Making matters worse, a political foe, Jacob Clingman, saw Hamilton leaving the Reynolds' home more than once. When confronted, Maria told him that Hamilton had been involved with her husband in some improper financial speculation.

Hamilton finally disentangled himself from the couple, making his last payment in June 1792. But rumors that he was covering up illegal speculation persisted. When Clingman brought letters implying just that to other politicians (including James Monroe), they confronted Hamilton. Eager to prove he had not compromised his role as Treasury secretary, he confessed to his private misdeeds. But though he asked the group to keep the truth secret, it eventually leaked. Some suspect the clerk who had copied Clingman's notes for Monroe. In 1797 a crude pamphleteer named James Thomson Callender publicly charged Hamilton with inappropriate behavior.

Hamilton had been accused of infidelity in print before, and his enduring reputation as a flirt made it easy to believe he had transgressed again. (In truth, there is no proof of his straying any other time in his marriage.) Furious that his public record was being besmirched, he went on the offensive. "The charge against me is a connection with one James Reynolds for the purposes of improper pecuniary speculation," he wrote in a 95-page

Hamilton had been accused of infidelity in print before, and his enduring reputation as a flirt made it easy to believe he had transgressed again.

OBSERVATIONS

ON

CERTAIN DOCUMENTS

"THE HISTORY OF THE UNITED STATES

CHARGE OF SPECULATION

ALEXANDER HAMILTON,

LATE SECRETARY OF THE TREASURY,

IS FULLY REFUTED.

WRITTEN BY HIMSELF.

PHILADELPHIA:

TABLOID TELL-ALL
The rakish Hamilton, desiring to reclaim his narrative amid financial scandal and allegations besmirching his character, admitted infidelity to Eliza in his "Reynolds Pamphlet."

booklet. "My real crime is an amorous connection with his wife, for a considerable time with his privity and connivance, if not originally brought on by a combination between the husband and wife with the design to extort money from me."

Revealing the details of the dalliance struck many as excessive, and Eliza must have been devastated by the attention. Alexander acknowledged as much in his booklet: "I can never cease to condemn myself for the pang which [this confession] may inflict in a bosom eminently entitled to all my gratitude, fidelity and love." Washington wrote a letter to Hamilton that conveyed his distress at seeing a friend in trouble without actually acknowledging the affair. The note accompanied a gift to Eliza: a four-bottle wine cooler that she treasured for the rest of her life.

Eliza was pregnant when the infidelity became public, and Hamilton held off on publishing his response until after she delivered their sixth child. For her part, Eliza never publicly commented on the scandal, and her husband's notes to her were still as sweet as ever. "I always feel how necessary you are to me," he wrote in 1798. "But when you are absent, I become still more sensible of it and look around in vain for that satisfaction which you alone can bestow."

For a while, the Hamiltons found renewed happiness and quietude in a new home in Upper Manhattan. But more tumult lay ahead. First, their son Philip was killed in a duel in 1801. Eliza was pregnant again and honored her fallen son by naming the baby Philip. Her eldest daughter, Angelica, took the loss particularly hard; she had a breakdown and never recovered. It's said she continued to speak of her brother as if he were alive.

Alexander must have had the tragedy in mind in the days leading up to his own duel three years later, taking pains to shield his family from the preparations. But there could be no avoiding the aftermath, particularly Eliza and the children having to say good-bye to him on his deathbed.

Eliza, who never remarried, found some comfort in a lock of hair clipped from her husband's head, and she wore around her neck a bag holding two pages: a sonnet her husband wrote to woo her and a hymn he left her on the morning of the duel. And as a new generation came to regard the widow as a fine piece of history, she took pleasure in regaling them with fond memories of "My Hamilton."

SIX THINGS YOU DIDN'T KNOW ABOUT HAMILTON

He was famous for his writings and his death, but there is a lot about his life that goes far beyond the headlines

BY DANIEL S. LEVY

1 He Could Have Been President

Yes, he was born outside the United States. But Alexander Hamilton still could have been president. Though the U.S. Constitution states that only "a natural born Citizen" can serve as commander in chief, it does include an exemption for anyone who was a "Citizen of the United States, at the time of the Adoption of this Constitution." In fact, in the late 18th and early 19th centuries, there were a slew of immigrants on such an elevated career trajectory. Besides Hamilton, there was Thomas Paine, the radical political journalist who gave hope to Gen. George Washington and his troops at Valley Forge with his *The American Crisis* pamphlet and its opening line, "These are the times that try men's souls." He hailed from Thetford, England. Albert Gallatin, the secretary of the Treasury who helped negotiate the end of the War of 1812 and co-founded New York University, was born in Geneva, Switzerland. Robert Morris, the banker known as the "financier of the American Revolution," left Liverpool, England, in 1747. And let us not forget Declaration of Independence signer James Wilson (Carskerdo, Scotland), U.S. Constitution framer William Paterson (County Antrim, Ireland), South Carolina senator Pierce Butler (County Carlow, Ireland) and Secretary of War James McHenry (Ballymena, Ireland), for whom Fort McHenry was named.

LOOPHOLE *Though not born in the colonies, Thomas Paine, above, and (clockwise from top left) James Wilson, Albert Gallatin, James McHenry and Robert Morris were among those who could have run for the nation's top office.*

2 He Was a Friend of the Jews

Johann Michael Lavien, the first husband of Hamilton's mother Rachel, may have been Jewish (in fact, his last name is likely a variation of *Levine*). If he was, though, he kept it a well-guarded secret, probably because such a lineage could have branded him unmarryable material. Tellingly, his son, Peter, Hamilton's half brother, was quietly baptized in his 20s, which suggests that he was trying to inoculate himself from his non-Christian ancestry. Still, Hamilton's contact with the Jews on Nevis—the first of whom arrived in the 17th century after being expelled from Brazil by the Portuguese—endeared him to his neighbors. And after being taught by a Jewish tutor who included Hebrew among his lessons, he developed a lifelong respect for the Jews, defending them at every chance: "Why distrust the evidence of the Jews? Discredit them and you destroy the Christian religion." The admiration was heartfelt. As he wrote, the "progress of the Jews ... from their earliest history to the present time has been and is entirely out of the ordinary course of human affairs. Is it not then, a fair conclusion that the cause is also an extraordinary one ...."

SACRED SITE *Some 2,500 Jews lived on Nevis when Hamilton was born, and they worshipped in the Charlestown Synagogue.*

THE STAIN OF SLAVERY *Hamilton abhorred the brutality of human bondage, and early on he sought to end it.*

3 He Was an Early Abolitionist

Growing up among sugar plantations, Hamilton saw firsthand the unfairness and brutality of slavery. In 1785 he, along with New York governor George Clinton, future Supreme Court chief justice John Jay and others, founded "The New-York Society for Promoting the Manumission of Slaves, and Protecting of Such of Them as have Been or May be Liberated." The men hoped to "excite the indignation of every friend to humanity" and sought to ban slavery. While Hamilton could not even get the society's members to agree to free their own slaves, the group worked hard for those with no rights. They published essays attacking the slave trade, kept a registry of blacks to protect them, and opened the African Free School, which offered an education to black children; before long, the institution was teaching hundreds. The society was among the anti-slavery organizations that petitioned Congress in 1791 to limit the trade in slaves, and though the effort failed, it paved the way for a 1799 law that was the first step toward the one eventually freeing all of New York's slaves by 1827.

4 He Stumbled Upon a Traitor

In early fall 1780, Gen. George Washington and a group of aides that included Hamilton headed to West Point—the future military academy—to perform an inspection. They had no reason to suspect that Gen. Benedict Arnold, the new commander of the post, would be less than a gracious host. But the brash war hero—he helped take Fort Ticonderoga and led troops in the battles of Lake Champlain and Saratoga—resented recently being passed over for a promotion. Worse, his lavish lifestyle had left him desperately short of money. So Arnold had secretly sold his allegiance to the British; in return for £20,000 and a high-level army commission, he passed along information about troop movements and promised to turn over the fort. As Hamilton and James McHenry waited for Washington at Arnold's headquarters a few miles from the fort, word came that Arnold's co-conspirator, British major John André, had been captured and maps of West Point had been found in his boot. A flustered but still unimplicated Arnold ran upstairs to see his wife, Margaret "Peggy" Shippen, and when Washington showed up, he and the others were left to wonder where Arnold had gone. Eventually, Washington left to inspect the fort, while Hamilton stayed behind. As he sorted through some papers, he heard cries from upstairs. There, he found an unhinged Peggy, holding her baby and talking incoherently. It was a convincing charade meant to disguise her complicity in her husband's crime. Meanwhile, Arnold had fled and was already on a British sloop-of-war appropriately christened *Vulture*. When Arnold's betrayal was made clear, Washington said, "Whom can we trust now?" To Hamilton, Arnold's actions were nothing less than "the blackest treason."

TREASON MOST FOUL *British major John André (above, right, with Benedict Arnold) was hanged after being discovered. Arnold and his wife, Peggy, left, escaped to live in London.*

LIQUID ASSET *The Great Falls of Paterson made the city a center of American industry.*

5 He Turned Water into Wealth

Paterson, N.J., is home to the Great Falls, a 77-foot-high waterfall that is the second largest east of the Mississippi River. Hamilton, who once lived nearby in Elizabethtown, knew the spot at the bend of the Passaic River. During a break from the war to have a "modest repast" of tongue, cold ham and biscuits in July 1778, he showed it off to Washington, McHenry and the Marquis de Lafayette. He understood the power-generating potential of the 2 billion gallons that tumbled over the falls each day. In 1791 he chartered the Society for Establishing Useful Manufactures (SUM) with financier William Duer and others. In its prospectus, the society noted that America could not "possess much active wealth but as the result of extensive manufactures." The organizers capitalized SUM at the exorbitant amount of $500,000 and named the nation's first planned industrial city in honor of New Jersey governor William Paterson. Pierre Charles L'Enfant, the designer of Washington, D.C., was tapped to figure out how to divert water from the falls, but his too-grand scheme was dismissed. His replacement, Peter Colt, dammed the ravine, formed a reservoir and created a path along which water could turn a mill. By 1794 the first cotton textile mill was up and running, and the city and nation were in business.

6 He Had Lots of Kids

Alexander and Elizabeth Schuyler Hamilton had eight children:

Philip The eldest Hamilton was named after his grandfather, Revolutionary general Philip Schuyler. In 1801 he got into an argument with George Eacker at the Park Theater and was fatally wounded in the subsequent duel—not far from the spot in New Jersey where his father would fall three years later.

Angelica Her brother's death caused her to have a nervous breakdown, and though her father tried to perk her up with gifts of parakeets and watermelons, she never improved and was an invalid until her death at 72.

Alexander Born in May 1786, he graduated from Columbia College. He learned military tactics in the Duke of Wellington's army in Portugal and served as a U.S. captain in the War of 1812. He became a U.S. district attorney in New York.

James Alexander He was a major in the War of 1812, was briefly acting secretary of state under President Andrew Jackson, and dealt in Manhattan real estate. As U.S. Attorney for the Southern District in New York, he was in the city when the Great Fire of 1835 hit, and he lit one of the fuses that blew up buildings to create a firebreak to help stop the blaze.

John Church He was an aide-de-camp to Gen. William Henry Harrison in the War of 1812 and edited his father's writing.

William Stephen The son who looked the most like his father fought in the Black Hawk War and was a U.S. surveyor of public lands in Illinois before heading to California in the gold rush.

Eliza She married Sidney Holley, and after his death she lived with her mother and helped maintain her father's papers.

Philip "Little Phil" was an assistant U.S. Attorney in New York and judge advocate of the U.S. Naval Retiring Board.

DEADLY PREVIEW *Hamilton's eldest child, Philip, was killed as his father would be, in a duel in New Jersey.*

THE FEDERALIST PAPERS: SELLING THE NEW CONSTITUTION

Developing a plan for a new government is no small feat; mustering public acceptance is even harder. Hamilton's arguments were so convincing, we refer to them still

BY RICHARD BEEMAN

ON MONDAY, SEPT. 17, 1787, WHEN Alexander Hamilton and 38 other delegates at the Constitutional Convention in Philadelphia stepped forward to sign a final draft of the document on which they had labored all summer, the words appearing on the four parchment sheets sitting on the table before them represented nothing more than opinion. At that point, the proposed Constitution lacked the sanction of the Continental Congress, the official governing body of the "united states." Nor had it achieved the approval of the governments of the 13 sovereign American states or of "We the people" residing in those states. By the terms of the proposal, the new government it described could take effect only after nine of the 13, deliberating in specially called ratifying conventions, added their assent.

Obtaining that assent would not be easy. All 13 of the states making up the fragile American union under the existing frame of government, the Articles of Confederation, were protective of the independence and sovereignty that they had achieved in the aftermath of the eight-year war with Great Britain. To varying degrees, those states were reluctant to yield any authority to a vastly strengthened central government. Moreover, because the delegates to the Philadelphia convention had carried out their proceedings in absolute secrecy, the sweeping changes they proposed would come as a shock to many of their countrymen.

The debate over the Constitution that followed was America's first national referendum—the first time voters in all of the states were asked to render a verdict. And the decision facing Americans couldn't have been starker: yes or no.

It was an intensely partisan contest. Supporters and opponents of ratification mounted campaign stumps in town and county meetings; local newspapers unleashed a deluge of often vitriolic equivalents of modern-day op-eds; and state and local politicians maneuvered behind the scenes to persuade the people of their states to elect either

CONFEDERATION *Persuading 13 independent states to agree on a codified statement of unity required a special man. Hamilton was that man.*

"Federalist" supporters of the Constitution or their "Anti-Federalist" opponents to each of the upcoming ratifying conventions. Between late September 1787 and the fall of 1788, several hundred pamphlets and newspaper essays expounded on the merits and demerits of the Constitution, the largest outpouring of opinion on any subject in the young country's history. Despite the partisan motives of all those pamphlets and essays, the ratification contest produced a body of political writing that achieved enduring intellectual importance.

Certainly the best-known and most influential of the work were the 85 essays written by Hamilton, James Madison and John Jay, each appearing under the single pseudonym "Publius" in New York City newspapers between October 1787 and May 1788 before being published together by John and Archibald McLean. Under the title of *The Federalist,* the first 36 essays became available on March 22, 1788, the rest on May 28, 1788.

The man most responsible for conceiving and organizing the effort was in one sense an unlikely choice for the job. Hamilton, though one of the signers of the Constitution, was not wholly pleased with the final product. He would have preferred a government based more closely on the aristocratic model of the English Constitution, and his contributions to the debates in the Constitutional Convention were, in the words of his fellow delegate William Samuel Johnson, "supported by none." But soon after the convention adjourned, Hamilton seized the moment, organizing a defense of the proposed Constitution against quickly mobilizing critics. He first attempted to recruit his friend and political ally Gouverneur Morris to collaborate with him on the essays. But Morris declined, so he turned to fellow New Yorker John Jay and, later, to James Madison. The choice of Madison—a key author of the Constitution—would have momentous consequences.

The man most responsible for conceiving The Federalist *essays was in one sense an unlikely choice for the job. Hamilton was not wholly pleased with the new Constitution.*

We the People

Article. 1

DONE IN CONVENTION *The U.S. Constitution was a product of extensive debate, deliberation and compromise.*

In all, Hamilton wrote 51 of the essays; Madison, 29; and Jay, five. (Jay might have made a greater contribution had he not taken ill after writing four of the first five pieces.) Most readers today tend to think of *The Federalist* as a single, consistent body of writing. Instead, the essays were written independently under great time pressure, so there was little opportunity for the authors to collaborate or review or revise one another's contributions. In fact, some scholars, aware of the bitter differences that later surfaced between Hamilton and Madison on matters of constitutional interpretation—with Hamilton in favor of a much more aggressive national government vis-à-vis the state governments—have detected a "split personality" in *The Federalist.*

But in the end, what is most striking from the perspective of the 21st century is the remarkable coherence of the essays. Whatever their future disagreements, Madison and Hamilton were able to forge a division of labor in the writing that minimized the possibility of individual differences emerging in print. In particular, Hamilton may

COLLECTIVE EFFORT *Statesman and diplomat John Jay, left, was prevented by illness from contributing more extensively to* The Federalist; *James Madison, right, lent the collection of essays a less partisan tone than Hamilton could pen.*

have deliberately muted his desire to create a national government that wielded even more power than the one conceived in Philadelphia. Similarly, he seems to have kept to himself concerns that the proposed government might be too much influenced by the passions of the people.

MANY OF THE ANTI-Federalist opponents of the Constitution feared precisely those things that Hamilton desired. Although they would not create a set of essays to match *The Federalist* in immediate impact or subsequent influence, Anti-Federalist writers did produce an impressive body of work, publishing more than 200 pamphlets, essays and broadsides. Because Anti-Federalist critics raised every objection they could devise in their attempt to defeat the ratification of the Constitution, their rhetoric sometimes lacked the intellectual coherence of *The Federalist.* But the broad themes of their critique—distrust of concentrated government power, empowering citizens to prevent government encroachments on individual liberty—have remained relevant to American constitutional and political discourse.

Another rallying point of the Anti-Federalists was a belief in the need to add a bill of rights to the proposed draft. Try as the Federalists did to argue that one was unnecessary, the Anti-Federalists understood that the public would not be persuaded without one. Indeed, had the Federalists not yielded on this point, promising to make the addition as soon as the new government commenced operation, it is likely that the Constitution would never have earned the nine votes necessary to secure its adoption. Moreover, without the Bill of Rights, our Constitution would have created a union considerably less "perfect" than the "more perfect" one promised in its preamble.

Ironically, the actual impact of *The Federalist* essays on the outcome of the ratification debate was likely limited. The essays did not circulate much beyond New York until the spring of 1788, so the voters in many states were not even familiar with the arguments put forth in them when they voted for their delegates. But over the course of America's subsequent history, *The Federalist* essays have reached the status of canonical text.

During the period between 1790 and 1800, when leaders of the new republic were engaging in passionate debates over how their new Constitution should be interpreted, *The Federalist* was cited in Supreme Court opinions only once. In the whole of the 19th century, the essays were cited 58 times, and in the first half of the 20th century 38 times. But in the last half of that century, there were no fewer than 196 citations. And if the first decade of

Americans who read The Federalist *are sure to gain a better understanding of the principles underlying our political system.*

the 21st century is a fair barometer, those 85 essays are becoming more important still. Some of the increased focus is almost certainly the consequence of the rising popularity of the doctrines of "originalism" and "original intent," as presented by Supreme Court justices such as Antonin Scalia and Clarence Thomas. The exceptionally articulate—on occasions brilliant—arguments in favor of the Constitution composed by Hamilton, Madison and Jay are tempting pieces of evidence for those who want to argue that constitutional interpretation should be constrained to "original meaning."

But the enduring value of *The Federalist* extends well beyond whatever practical utility the essays may have in settling constitutional disputes today. Although Hamilton, Madison and Jay conceived of the essays in the context of an 18th-century world and in the heat of partisan battle, their insights about law, government, culture and human nature retain a timeless quality. Americans who read *The Federalist* are sure to gain a better understanding of the principles underlying our political system and, therefore, a better understanding of our rights and responsibilities as citizens.

Whatever Hamilton's brilliance, it is most often Madison who is referred to as "the Father of the Constitution." One of the reasons Madison's essays have gained proportionally more attention (Madison wrote only slightly more than a third of the essays) is that many of Hamilton's essays were more partisan in tone. Appearing early in the series, they were aimed at pointing out the weaknesses of the existing Articles of Confederation and refuting the arguments of Anti-Federalist opponents. These were important considerations when the essays were written, but they have become less so over time. Further, as America's constitutional history has unfolded, it has tended to be the Madisonian, rather than the Hamiltonian, view of vitally important issues such as federalism, separation of powers, and checks and balances that has come to dominate political thought.

It was appropriate that Hamilton, as the organizer of the enterprise, took the lead on most of the early essays, writing 27 of the first 36. (Madison then took over, writing 22 consecutive essays, from *Federalist 37* to *Federalist 58*, after which Hamilton took charge again, writing 24 of the remaining 27.)

Hamilton's *Federalist 1* served both as an introduction to the larger work and as an appeal to the people to place the broader "public good" ahead of what he described as the "interested or ambitious views" of many opponents of the Constitution. This would be a recurring theme in Hamilton's essays, often accompanied by an aggressive defense of the virtues of an "energetic" government and a recitation of the dangers of a weak and divided nation. In *Federalist 6*, for example, he warned of the threat that "separate confederacies" might pose to the nation at large, and in *Federalist 15*, he answered the Anti-Federalists' arguments against a "consolidated" government with a passionate enumeration of the ways in which the misdeeds of individual state governments posed a greater threat to the public good than any imagined fears about the excessive power of a national government. Expanding further in *Federalist 23*, he again defended the virtues of an "energetic" central government while adding an argument for the creation of a standing army—a source of great fear among some Anti-Federalists—to provide for the common defense. It is in essays like *Federalist 15* and *23* that we see Hamilton at his most partisan.

MADISON MADE HIS ENtrance as "Publius" with a bang, writing what has become the most famous of all of the *Federalist* essays, *Number 10*, in which he embarked on a distinctly modern approach to the existence of "faction" and "interests" in American politics. Whereas most 18th-century commentators believed that the key to good government was to elect virtuous political leaders capable of transcending narrow self-interest, Madison accepted the existence of conflicting interests as an inherent part of any society. Turning prevailing wisdom about politics and government on its head, Madison argued that the best way to control the effects of faction was to extend the sphere of government over a sufficiently large territory so that no one faction could gain undue influence and subvert the public good. Madison continued with this logic in *Federalist 14*, arguing that an "extended

FEDERALISM DEFENSE *From his days as a student at King's College, above, Hamilton was distrustful of mob mentality, so it is no surprise that he later argued for a strong government to temper the power of the people.*

republic," such as that in America, based as it was on the principle of representation, was in many ways preferable to a direct democracy, such as that of ancient Athens, in which the people themselves "meet and exercise the government in person."

It was in *37* through *58* that Madison really hit his stride. These essays deal with some of the most important issues in American government—republicanism, federalism, separation of powers, and checks and balances. Of these essays, two of the most important are numbers *39*, in which Madison describes the proposed new government as being "part national" and "part federal" in character, and *51*, in which he embarks on a brilliant exposition, continued in subsequent essays, on the principles of separation of powers and checks and balances.

Jay recovered from his illness long enough to pen *Number 64*, in which he discusses the treaty-making power of the proposed U.S. Senate—a subject on which he was extremely knowledgeable, as he had been one of the principal negotiators of the treaty of peace with England that formally ended the Revolutionary War.

Hamilton took over from there. The most important of his concluding essays was *Number 78*, probably his most significant contribution to *The Federalist*. Arguing for the importance of protecting "the weakest of the three departments of government," the judiciary, he defended the provision calling for the appointment of federal judges during a term of "good behavior," that is, lifetime service barring any disqualifying actions. In the process of defending that provision, Hamilton went on to argue that "the interpretation of the laws is the proper and peculiar province of the courts. A constitution is in fact, and must be, regarded by the judges as the fundamental law. It therefore belongs to them to ascertain its meaning as well as the meaning of any law proceeding from the legislative body." The judiciary's power of "judicial review" would not be established as a constitutional precedent until the Supreme Court rendered its decision in *Marbury v. Madison* in 1803, but Hamilton's argument in *Federalist 78* was a crucial portent of constitutional developments to come.

The authors of *The Federalist*, along with many of their counterparts on both sides of the issue of ratification, would not have been so presumptuous as to describe themselves as "political thinkers." But they were, in the best sense of the phrase, "thinking politicians." As historian Gordon Wood has observed, they were writing at a point in history when intellectualism and political activism could naturally coexist. They brought to their work as public officials and political activists an impressive understanding of history and of political philosophy. No wonder that their essays have transcended their original, partisan purpose. Indeed, one can only hope that they will continue to serve as a model for contemporary politicians and journalists to emulate.

HIGHLIGHTS OF *THE FEDERALIST PAPERS*

Between them, Hamilton, James Madison and John Jay wrote 85 essays to sway the ratification debate in favor of the proposed Constitution. Some of those essays were bound to be more relevant and longer-lasting than others. For instance, the three excerpted below.

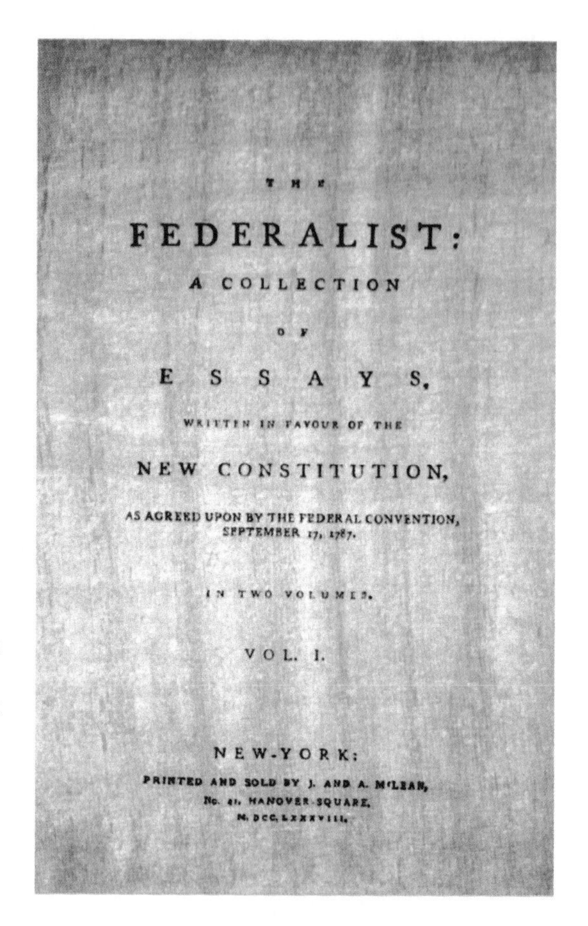
THE
FEDERALIST:
A COLLECTION
OF
ESSAYS,
WRITTEN IN FAVOUR OF THE
NEW CONSTITUTION,
AS AGREED UPON BY THE FEDERAL CONVENTION,
SEPTEMBER 17, 1787.
IN TWO VOLUMES.
VOL. I.
NEW-YORK:
PRINTED AND SOLD BY J. AND A. M'LEAN,
No. 41, HANOVER-SQUARE.
M,DCC,LXXXVIII.

Federalist No. 1

Oct. 27, 1787

After an unequivocal experience of the inefficacy of the subsisting Foederal Government, you are called upon to deliberate on a new Constitution for the United States of America. The Subject speaks its own importance; comprehending in its consequences, nothing less than the existence of the UNION, the safety and welfare of the parts of which it is composed, the fate of an empire, in many respects, the most interesting in the world. It has been frequently remarked, that it seems to have been reserved to the people of this country, by their conduct and example, to decide the important question, whether societies of men are really capable or not, of establishing good government from reflection and choice, or whether they are forever destined to depend, for their political constitutions, on accident and force. If there be any truth in the remark, the crisis, at which we are arrived, may with propriety be regarded as the era in which that decision is to be made; and a wrong election of the part we shall act, may, in this view, deserve to be considered as the general misfortune of mankind.

This idea will add the inducements of philanthropy to those of patriotism to heighten the solicitude, which all considerate and good men must feel for the event. Happy will it be if our choice should be directed by a judicious estimate of our true interests, unperplexed and unbiased by considerations not connected with the public good. But this is a thing more ardently to be wished, than seriously to be expected. The plan offered to our deliberations, affects too many particular interests, innovates upon too many local institutions, not to involve in its discussion a variety of objects foreign to its merits, and of views, passions and prejudices little favourable to the discovery of truth.

★ ★ ★

I propose in a series of papers to discuss the following interesting particulars—the utility of the UNION to your political prosperity—The insufficiency of the present Confederation to preserve that Union—The necessity of a government at least equally energetic with the one proposed to the attainment of this object—The conformity of the proposed constitution to the true principles of republican government—Its analogy to your own state constitution—and lastly, The additional security, which its adoption will afford to the preservation of that species of government, to liberty and to property.

In the progress of this discussion I shall endeavour to give a satisfactory answer to all the objections which shall have made their appearance that may seem to have any claim to your attention. It may perhaps be thought superfluous to offer arguments to prove the utility of the UNION, a point, no doubt, deeply engraved on the hearts of the great body of the people in every state, and one, which it may be imagined has no adversaries. But the fact is, that we already hear it whispered in the private circles of those who oppose the new constitution, that the Thirteen States are of too great extent for any general system, and that we must of necessity resort to separate confederacies of distinct portions of the whole. This doctrine will, in all probability, be gradually propagated, till it has votaries enough to countenance an open avowal of it. For nothing can be more evident, to those who are able to take an enlarged view of the subject, than the alternative of an adoption of the new Constitution, or a dismemberment of the Union. It will therefore be of use to begin by examining the advantages of that Union, the certain evils and the probable dangers, to which every State will be exposed from its dissolution. This shall accordingly constitute the subject of my next address.

Federalist No. 23

Dec. 18, 1787

The necessity of a Constitution, at least equally energetic with the one proposed, to the preservation of the Union, is the point, at the examination of which we are now arrived.

This enquiry will naturally divide itself into three branches—the objects to be provided for by a Foederal Government—the quantity of power necessary to the accomplishment of those objects—the persons upon whom that power ought to operate. Its distribution and organization will more properly claim our attention under the succeeding head.

The principal purposes to be answered by Union are these—The common defence of the members—the preservation of the public peace as well against internal convulsions as external attacks—the regulation of commerce with other nations and between the States—the superintendence of our intercourse, political and commercial, with foreign countries.

The authorities essential to the care of the common defence are these—to raise armies—to build and equip fleets—to prescribe rules for the government of both—to direct their operations—to provide for their support. These powers ought to exist without limitation: Because it is impossible to foresee or define the extent and variety of national exigencies, or the correspondent extent & variety of the means which may be necessary to satisfy them. The circumstances that endanger the safety of nations are infinite; and for this reason no constitutional shackles can wisely be imposed on the power to which the care of it is committed. This power ought to be co-extensive with all the possible combinations of such circumstances; and ought to be under the direction of the same councils, which are appointed to preside over the common defence.

★ ★ ★

I flatter myself, that the observations which have been made in the course of these papers, have sufficed to place the reverse of that position in as clear a light as any matter still in the womb of time and experience can be susceptible of. This at all events must be evident, that the very difficulty itself drawn from the extent of the country, is the strongest argument in favor of an energetic government; for any other can certainly never preserve the Union of so large an empire. If we embrace the tenets of those, who oppose the adoption of the proposed Constitution, as the standard of our political creed, we cannot fail to verify the gloomy doctrines, which predict the impracticability of a national system, pervading the entire limits of the present Confederacy.

Federalist No. 78

May 28, 1788

Whoever attentively considers the different departments of power must perceive, that in a government in which they are separated from each other, the judiciary, from the nature of its functions, will always be the least dangerous to the political rights of the constitution; because it will be least in a capacity to annoy or injure them. The executive not only dispenses the honors, but holds the sword of the community. The legislature not only commands the purse, but prescribes the rules by which the duties and rights of every citizen are to be regulated. The judiciary on the contrary has no influence over either the sword or the purse, no direction either of the strength or of the wealth of the society, and can take no active resolution whatever. It may truly be said to have neither Force nor Will, but merely judgment; and must ultimately depend upon the aid of the executive arm even for the efficacy of its judgments.

This simple view of the matter suggests several important consequences. It proves incontestably that the judiciary is beyond comparison the weakest of the three departments of power; that it can never attack with success either of the other two; and that all possible care is requisite to enable it to defend itself against their attacks. It equally proves, that though individual oppression may now and then proceed from the courts of justice, the general liberty of the people can never be endangered from that quarter: I mean, so long as the judiciary remains truly distinct from both the legislative and executive. For I agree that "there is no liberty, if the power of judging be not separated from the legislative and executive powers" [Montesquieu, *The Spirit of the Laws*]. And it proves, in the last place, that as liberty can have nothing to fear from the judiciary alone, but would have every thing to fear from its union with either of the other departments.

HAMILTON AND JEFFERSON: THE

When two powerful and profound political thinkers fundamentally disagree

RIVALRY THAT FORGED A NATION

about the nature of things, one perspective has to lose. Unless everybody wins BY JOHN FERLING

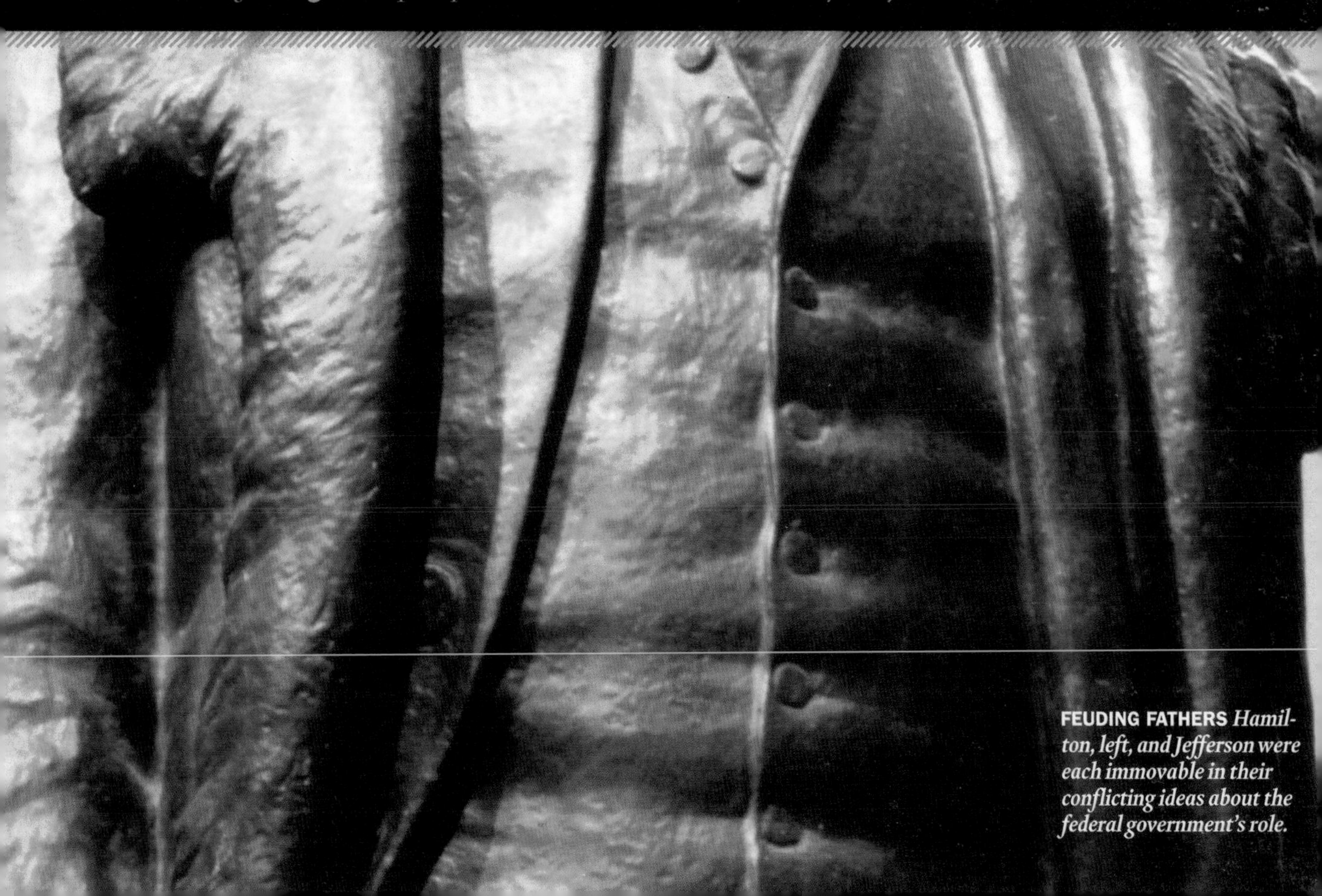

FEUDING FATHERS *Hamilton, left, and Jefferson were each immovable in their conflicting ideas about the federal government's role.*

"Hamilton & myself were daily pitted in the cabinet like two cocks." —THOMAS JEFFERSON

THINK GREAT AMERICAN RIVALRIES, and Lincoln-Douglas or LBJ-RFK or maybe even Bill Gates–Steve Jobs jumps to mind. But none of those—or any others, for that matter—were as fervent, and certainly none were more consequential, than the competitive coexistence of Alexander Hamilton and Thomas Jefferson.

Though they may have been sparring over economic and foreign policy issues like so many politicians who succeeded them, nothing less than the shape of a new nation was at stake. And both of them knew it.

Before George Washington appointed them to his cabinet—Hamilton as Treasury secretary, Jefferson as secretary of state—they barely even knew of one another. (They may have met briefly a decade earlier.) Jefferson had spent the second half of the 1780s overseas, as Minister to France, before reluctantly accepting Washington's call and making his way to New York, the country's capital, in the spring of 1790. By that time, Hamilton had already been at his post for more than seven months. Jefferson arrived in Manhattan aware that Hamilton favored a stronger national government, but Hamilton had little idea where Jefferson stood on the questions of the day. After five years abroad, Jefferson did not know either, telling James Madison that he was unfamiliar with both the issues and many of the new political players who had emerged in post-Revolutionary America.

Initially, the two men enjoyed a cordial relationship. Jefferson invited Hamilton to dinner on a couple of occasions, and they seldom clashed during their first year in the administration. But they were never close. A dozen years apart in age—Jefferson was 47 and Hamilton 35 in 1790—they could not have been more different in temperament. Hamilton was outgoing and outspoken; he dominated every room. Jefferson, amiable and erudite, was quiet and reserved.

It was deep philosophical differences, though, that soon set them against each other. Jefferson had been driven to champion revolution by Britain's onerous policies. But like Thomas Paine, who in *Common Sense* had portrayed the American Revolution as a chance to begin "the world over again," he primarily saw the country's independence as an occasion to bring changes to his home state of Virginia. Specifically, he wanted to end the political stranglehold of the planter elite and offer religious liberty and greater opportunity to all free Virginians. In place of a monarchy and aristocracy—to his mind, the perpetrators of "treason" against humankind—he sought to install a democratic commonwealth.

What Jefferson saw in Europe had only deepened his ardor for change. Traveling widely, he found so much of humanity mired in poverty and hopelessness. Capricious monarchs and aristocrats, living in obscene luxury, suppressed the common people to preserve their power and privilege. "I was much an enemy to monarchy before I came to Europe. I am ten thousand times more so since I have seen what they are," wrote Jefferson. He rejoiced when the French Revolution began in 1789, counting on it not only to transform France but to spark similar rebellions across the continent as well.

HAMILTON DID NOT SHARE Jefferson's radicalism. Though he too objected to Parliament's exploitation of the colonists, he ascribed it to a conspiracy of a "few artful men" rather than any deep-rooted flaws in the system. And while he favored independence—and had fought for it passionately—he was leery of social upheaval.

The Revolutionary War, in fact, was crucial to forging Hamilton's outlook. As Washington's closest aide, he saw firsthand the daily misery of the soldiers and the overall, near-fatal, weakness of the military, and blamed both on the collapse of the national economy under the watch of a feeble Continental Congress. In his "Continentalist" essays from 1780, Hamilton, asserting that weak government leads inevitably to "the ruin of the people," advocated for giving greater powers to Congress.

Though America miraculously overcame its

A UNITER *George Washington spent parts of his presidency mediating between his two battling cabinet members.*

military shortcomings to defeat the British, the country remained in a precarious economic condition. As political ferment roiled throughout the states in the unsettled postwar period, newcomers elbowed their way into positions of influence, to the alarm of the old colonial elite. Hamilton deplored the democratic upsurge that gave authority to this "leveling kind." For him, only supremacy of the national government over the states could assure that the "power of government is entrusted to proper hands." In a remarkably candid speech at the Constitutional Convention, Hamilton urged the "formal Extinction of State Governments" and the establishment of a national regime that replicated Great Britain's, calling it "the best model the world ever produced."

IN JEFFERSON'S VIEW, CENTRALized government was simply European-style tyranny waiting to happen again. Informed by his upbringing in agrarian Virginia, he dreamed of a society of property-owning farmers who controlled their destiny. While a manufacturing economy was driven by avarice, a republic resting on the yeoman farmer would keep "alive that sacred fire" of personal liberty and virtue.

Hamilton, of course, had risen meteorically in the world of urban commerce. Naturally, he believed that a flourishing merchant economy would sow opportunities for all. Further, it would produce a philanthropic, knowledgeable and enterprising people. Jefferson once equated cities with "great sores," but in Hamilton's eyes they were focal points of societal health, providing a foundation for wealth creation, consumerism, the arts, innovation and enlightenment. A clash between the two Founding Fathers was inevitable.

The economic program instituted by the Treasury secretary triggered Jefferson's suspicions, but it wasn't until he learned what Hamilton had preached at the Constitutional Convention that he put together the whole puzzle. He saw as dangerous Hamilton's push to strengthen the central government and presidency. And he detected an intent to secure the sway of the "financial interest" over Congress and foster the growth of a new moneyed class. All of it would menace republicanism and the agrarian way of life. Jefferson was sure that before long, Hamiltonianism would produce in America the same evil cause-and-effects he had witnessed in Europe: monarchy and rigid social stratification leading to massive poverty and widespread urban squalor.

He responded by organizing the Republican Party. Jefferson also hired Philip Freneau, a gifted writer with a penchant for satire, to run an opposition newspaper, the *National Gazette.* And he denounced Hamilton to Washington, reporting that his rival had praised Britain's government while calling the Constitution a "shilly shally thing" destined to be replaced by something better. Hamilton, Jefferson warned, secretly schemed to restore monarchy in America. Already, a "corrupt squadron" of Hamiltonians within Congress was engaged in financial speculation, disdaining constitutional limits on government's power. Washington, though, was unmoved; he believed in his former aide and the economic path he had set, one that would leave the country "prosperous & happy."

Hamilton countered Jefferson's attacks by establishing his own party, the Federalists. He denied plotting an American monarchy, saying that only a "madman" would attempt such a thing, and suggested to Washington that Jefferson was the one with designs—to be president and eradicate the current economic program. It was Jefferson too, driven by "violent passions" and an "unsound & dangerous" philosophy, who wanted to displace the Constitution.

BUT EVEN AS THE PAIR FOUGHT relentlessly, they agreed on two issues. When Washington spoke of retiring after one term, both men beseeched him to continue. And when the French Revolution led to a broader European war, the two were of one mind in thinking America must remain neutral. In 1793, though, Britain was lured into the overseas conflict, arousing passions in the States that domestic issues "could never excite," as Jefferson remarked. Hamilton, who understood trade with England to be crucial to the nation's economy, counseled support of Britain. In Jefferson's opinion, Hamilton was "panick struck" by the pro-French sentiment that prevailed in America. He, in turn, was invigorated by the support, seeing it as a sign that "the old spirit of 1776 is rekindling." In short, he saw it as proof that the days of Hamiltonianism were numbered.

Jefferson left the cabinet and retired from public life in 1794. Hamilton followed a year later. Convinced that the "philosopher of Monticello" remained obsessed with becoming president, Hamilton never expected the retirement to last. Still, during Jefferson's three years away, Hamilton said little in public about his rival, even remaining silent when rumors circulated of Jefferson's alleged sexual relationship with one of his female slaves. Nor did Jefferson comment when Hamilton's extramarital affair with Maria Reynolds became public in 1797.

From Monticello, his Virginia estate, a concerned Jefferson kept watch on the presidency. When Washington raised an army to crush defiant western farmers who opposed an excise tax on whiskey—a tax Hamilton had proposed—Jefferson privately condemned the "inexcusable aggression" against "people at their ploughs" and guessed correctly that Hamilton had been a proponent of the use of force. In 1795, Washington signed the Jay Treaty, a pact with England that clearly aligned the U.S. with their onetime governors; Hamilton was a principal supporter of the accord. For the effort, Jefferson called him the "servile copyist of Mr. Pitt," England's prime minister, and concluded that Washington had become a Federalist in fact if not in name. Unlike many others, though, Jefferson never intimated that Hamilton had manipulated the president. Instead, he praised his rival's persuasive and polemical skills. "Hamilton is really a colossus" of his party, he conceded.

As Hamilton predicted, his rival did run for president, in 1796. Throughout the campaign, Jefferson endured furious assaults by the Federalists, who portrayed him as a hypocrite—an elitist who insincerely spouted notions of equality. Jefferson lost, to John Adams, and had to settle for the vice presidency. Two years later, events transpired that troubled him more than anything had since Hamilton's economic policies. Spurred by America's "cold war" with France, Congress enacted the Alien and Sedition Acts, repressive measures designed by the Federalists, including Hamilton. Jefferson called the legislation "detestable" and "worthy of the 8th or 9th century" and deemed the Federalist government a "reign of witches." That reign grew scarier still when Congress ordered the creation of a large standing army, which Hamilton, with Washington's help, commanded. Proclaiming Hamilton "our Buonaparte," Jefferson predicted the federal troops would be used

SELF-EVIDENT TRUTHS *President Jefferson presents the Declaration of Independence he had drafted years earlier.*

against domestic dissidents. (On this point, he was not wholly wrong: Hamilton said in private that he would not hesitate to "subdue a refractory and powerful state.")

JEFFERSON RAN FOR PRESIDENT again in 1800, and this time Hamilton, more consumed with defeating John Adams, whom he both hated and could not exploit, said little against his political enemy. And when the election ended in a tie with Aaron Burr, Hamilton supported Jefferson, arguing that he was "able and wise" though his political philosophy was "tinctured with fanaticism." Almost as soon as the tie was broken in Jefferson's favor, though, Hamilton reverted to his adversarial ways. In several newspaper pieces, he contended that the new president meant to destroy the Constitution. Jefferson ignored the onslaught, perhaps having concluded that Hamilton and his faction were a spent force.

Within four years, Hamilton would be dead, but Jefferson did not exult. And to the end he

Almost as soon as the tie was broken in Jefferson's favor, Hamilton reverted to his adversarial ways. In several newspaper pieces, he contended that the new president meant to destroy the Constitution.

spoke only generously of his foe. The two had "thought well" of one another, he said. Moreover, Hamilton was "a singular character" of "acute understanding," a man who had been "disinterested, honest, and honorable."

Jefferson called his election the "revolution of 1800," and over the next quarter century much of the world that he first envisioned in 1776 took shape: the United States was cast as an egalitarian democracy that effectively erased the social hierarchies of the colonies, and with federal land easier to purchase, the percentage of the labor force involved in farming increased.

Hamilton, of course, would have been dismayed by much of the change. In his final letter, he wrote that "our real Disease . . . is Democracy." (To bolster his point, he also called it a "poison.") But he would have rejoiced at America's transformation into a modern capitalist society. Within 20 years of his death, cities were expanding and banks had sprung up like weeds. In countless Northeast towns, residents were more likely to work in a factory than to own a farm.

It is safe to say that aside from George Washington himself, no one had a greater impact on the founding and development of our nation than Hamilton and Jefferson. Their opposing visions wind like the twin strands of DNA through American history. Jefferson was the more revolutionary of the two, and his ringing affirmation of human rights in the Declaration of Independence has inspired much of the world for more than two centuries. But Hamilton laid the foundation for the strong, centralized modern state led by a powerful executive. The footprints of the two rivals remain visible across the globe, but today's America more clearly bears the mark of Hamilton.

John Ferling is the author of Jefferson and Hamilton: The Rivalry That Forged a Nation, *from which this piece is adapted.*

READ ALL ABOUT IT: THE STORY OF THE *NEW YORK POST*

Founded to spotlight his Federalist views, Hamilton's paper has survived one name change, several owners and a gamut of ideologies

BY ELLEN TUMPOSKY

THE *NEW YORK POST* WAS FOUNDED FOR reasons that might resonate with its current publisher: to advance a political agenda and skewer anyone who disagreed with it. In its first edition, on Nov. 16, 1801, the *New-York Evening Post* promised to print only worthy stories: "The design of this paper is to diffuse among the people correct information on all interesting subjects, to inculcate just principles in religion, morals and politics; and to cultivate a taste for sound literature." In reality, though, the newspaper was zealously committed to advancing the views of the Federalist Party at the expense of the Democratic-Republicans, the party of President Thomas Jefferson.

The daily newspaper's guiding principle was largely the brainchild of Alexander Hamilton. He conceived the enterprise with a group of staunch political allies who loathed the anti-Federalist climate in both New York State and Washington, D.C. Each of the founders was asked to invest at least $100; for his part, Hamilton may have pitched in as much as $1,000 to the total capitalization of about $10,000. Early readers, including such illustrious New Yorkers as merchant John Jacob Astor and banker Anthony Bleecker, paid a hefty $8 for a yearly subscription; the paper was not sold to the rabble in the streets.

The *Evening Post* was only a week old when it was forced to cover one of the most tragic events of Hamilton's life: the death of his beloved son Philip in a duel with a 27-year-old lawyer and Jefferson supporter, George Eacker. According to Ron Chernow's biography of Hamilton, Philip had been counseled by his father to either shoot into the air or avoid firing altogether, so that if he were killed it would be viewed as a homicide. And that's how the paper depicted the event: as Eacker having "murdered" the 19-year-old man (while neglecting to mention that Philip had fired too).

Hamilton, a prolific writer, contributed only one bylined piece to the *Evening Post*—a rebuttal to a report that at the Battle of Yorktown during the Revolutionary War, the Marquis de Lafayette had ordered Hamilton to execute British prisoners. But he authored 18 pro-Federalist pieces under the pen name Lucius Crassus, all of them vigorous attacks on Jefferson. The president was later described in the paper in language as spiteful as any found in

NEW YORK POST

LATE CITY FINAL

TUESDAY, MARCH 16, 1993 / Sunny, 40-45 today; cloudy, chance of rain, upper 30s tonight / Details, Page 2

50¢

FOUNDED IN 1801 BY ALEXANDER HAMILTON

TABLOID TURMOIL *A period of disorder in March 1993 led* Post *staffers to revolt against the paper's then owner with a front-page image of a weeping Hamilton.*

today's gossip columns: "dressed in long boots, with tops turned down about the ankles, like a Virginia buck; overalls of corduroy, faded by frequent immersions in soapsuds from a yellow to a dull white; . . . linen very considerably soiled; hair uncombed and beard unshaven."

AFTER HAMILTON EERILY followed his son's fate in 1804, felled in a duel with Aaron Burr, the *Evening Post* continued its mission under William Coleman, a former Massachusetts state legislator and the original editor of the paper. He moved the paper away from its Federalist partnership and backed Democrat Andrew Jackson. The romantic poet William Cullen Bryant took over the paper in 1827 and supported Abraham Lincoln, a Republican, on an anti-slavery platform.

The paper passed through various hands, becoming conservative in the early 20th century. Then in 1939, Dorothy Schiff, the daughter of a wealthy banking family, purchased it and installed her husband George Backer as publisher. "Dolly" Schiff soon divorced Backer, though, and married the features editor. Together, they turned the venerable broadsheet into a tabloid in 1942, and Schiff became media fodder in her own right. The *New York Times* wrote that she "looks younger than her 39 years and wears really feminine clothes," and it quoted her populist self-assessment, "I enjoy the play every one raves about and I like the book every one is reading."

Schiff's *Post* was fiercely liberal—resisting pressures to rein in its left-leaning writers during the McCarthyite 1950s—until its run ended abruptly in 1976, when Australian media magnate Rupert Murdoch acquired the paper and pulled its editorial stance way to the right while remaking it as a sassy, down-market British-style tabloid. Murdoch gave up control of the *Post* just over 11 years later, and it was bought by a real estate developer, Peter Kalikow, who hung on until 1993. In quick succession, ownership and management ricocheted from a rogue financier to a buffoonish parking-garage magnate and ultimately back to Murdoch. At one point the paper's distressed staff produced a front page that featured Hamilton with a tear rolling down his cheek.

It's unlikely that Hamilton—himself a target of scandalmongers when he conducted a high-profile adulterous affair—would be shocked by the 21st-century *Post*. Rather, he'd be mystified by the modern "objective" press. Alexander Hamilton wouldn't have seen the point of a paper without a point of view.

Ellen Tumposky is a writer and editor who has reported for People, *the* New York Daily News *and* USA Today.

MONEY IS POWER: HOW HAMILTON'S FINANCIAL VISION LIVES ON

A strong centralized banking system was crucial to Hamilton's framework for America's growth and prosperity. Here's how he made it happen

BY CHRISTOPHER MATTHEWS

America's financial system is the most powerful and stable in the world. You effectively can't do business internationally without also doing business with the biggest American banks and the U.S. central bank, the Federal Reserve. But history did not have to unfold this way. Some of the most influential Founding Fathers and framers of the Constitution, from Thomas Jefferson to John Adams to James Madison, were deeply suspicious of banks and fought hard to shield the new republic from their influence. Alexander Hamilton was nearly alone among the intellectual powerhouses of the early republic in his defense of a vigorous banking system as necessary not only for the economic security of the nation but for the full flowering of its people. In 1776 the U.S. was an overwhelmingly agricultural nation. A large majority of the delegates to the Constitutional Convention were farmers whose relationship to banks and bankers was adversarial. Many of America's Founding Fathers, therefore, were wary of finance and banking. Their philosophy derived in part from personal experience. Thomas Jefferson fought his whole life to stay one step ahead of his debt collectors.

But Alexander Hamilton's pedigree as the poor, propertyless son of a single mother offered him another perspective on banking and money and how these tools might be used to bring prosperity to a young nation. After Hamilton's mother died, he was taken under the wing of a successful St. Croix merchant, Thomas Stevens. As Stevens's apprentice, Hamilton dove headfirst into a world of multinational commerce. In the 18th century, the islands of the Caribbean were the crossroads of empires, where European powers competed with one another to enrich themselves through the trade of commodities and slaves. It was also a place where a boy of Hamilton's social standing was able to see firsthand the grinding poverty that an agricultural economy forced on people, most especially the vast slave class, without whom extracting sugar and other commodities from the land would not have been profitable.

During the Revolutionary War, Hamilton served as a captain in the army and an aide-de-camp to Gen. George Washington. That experience too taught him much about economics and inter-

national relations, as the American army suffered greatly from the fact that England's mercantilist policies forced the colonies to produce only raw materials from the land and to buy more advanced products, like munitions and textiles, from England itself. Not only was fostering a modern economy capable of producing such goods important for promoting prosperity, it was a national-security imperative.

ROBERT MORRIS *The merchant and politician shared Hamilton's vision for a national bank.*

Equally problematic for the young United States of America was the ruinous inflation these shortages of goods, in combination with the overprinting of paper money, wrought on the U.S. economy. As a 25-year-old officer in the war, Hamilton had an understanding of monetary theory that was impressive both for his young age and for the fact that economics as a field of study didn't even exist as we understand it today. The foundational text of Western economics, Adam Smith's *The Wealth of Nations*, was first published in 1776, the year America declared independence. Through study of such works and his own trenchant observations, Hamilton understood that inflation was not just the result of shortages of staple goods and an oversupply of money; it had a psychological component as well.

FINALLY, EVEN BEFORE THE war ended, Hamilton saw that the young republic would be crippled by debt if the federal government weren't given the tools to promote and manage the nation's credit.

The solution to these problems was in part the creation of a national banking system that was privately owned but overseen by the federal government through a central bank. As early as 1781, Hamilton was arguing cogently that the power of the British empire was underwritten not so much by its formidable navy but by a "vast fabric of credit," as he wrote in a letter to Robert Morris, the U.S. superintendent of finance. It was Britain's vigorous financial system, amplified by the deft management of public debt, that enabled the empire to project power farther than any other nation.

Hamilton's correspondence with Morris shows that even during the war, when his days were occupied with the nuts and bolts of the American war effort, he had the mental acuity to continue to master the subjects of international relations and high finance. In his letter to Morris, he argued forcefully for a central bank that could help shoulder the financing of the Revolutionary War effort and turn American sovereign debt from a burden to an advantage. "A national debt, if it is not excessive, will be to us a national blessing. It will be a powerful cement of our union," Hamilton wrote.

Morris was impressed with the Hamiltonian worldview and was in a position to help carry out these ideas. Morris, who made his riches in the slave trade, also understood the need for ample credit to grease the wheels of commerce and to fund the war effort. He successfully petitioned the Continental Congress to establish the Bank of North America to lend money to the fledgling federal government to buy munitions and pay troops. The bank, which the Continental Congress chartered in 1781, was a critical tool in funneling private capital and loans from the French government toward the war effort.

Though the Bank of North America was an essential institution for helping the U.S. win the Revolutionary War, the Articles of Confederation that bound the states together did not arrange the right conditions for capitalism and economic growth. State property laws were weak and in conflict with one another. Since the individual states all issued competing coinage, merchants had to contend with a confusing array of currencies and changing exchange rates, while inflationary forces put a damper on economic activity overall.

To help right the ship in New York State, Hamilton was chosen by leading local business leaders to draft the constitution of the Bank of New York, which launched in 1784. The establishment of the bank provided new capital for New York business ventures and smoothed commerce by providing another option, Bank of New York notes, to use as currency. As Hamilton biographer Ron Chernow wrote of his Bank of New York charter, "The resulting document was taken up as the pattern for many subsequent bank charters and helped to define the rudiments of American banking."

The Bank of New York brought some degree of order and prosperity to New York City while helping the city gain a few lengths in the race to be-

ON SOLID GROUND *The establishment of the First Bank of the United States on Third Street in Philadelphia, with its expansion of the federal government's role in economic policy, made tangible Hamilton's Federalist worldview.*

come America's preeminent commercial city. But Hamilton knew that for his vision of the U.S. financial system to come to fruition, it would require the establishment of a strong central authority that could raise debt and establish a central bank in the English model.

The path from the Bank of New York to the First Bank of the United States took Hamilton to the Constitutional Convention, where he successfully advocated for powers like the commerce clause and the necessary-and-proper clause, which gave the federal government the power to coordinate economic policy across the states and to take actions necessary for fulfilling its Constitutional role. After President George Washington appointed Hamilton as the nation's first Treasury secretary, he used those newly enumerated powers to almost single-handedly forge a partnership between the public sector and private banks that would bind the country together and attract the capital to power the young nation's economy.

The first step was winning a political battle over the question of whether the federal government should assume the war debts of the individual states. The nascent Democratic-Republican faction, led by Secretary of State Thomas Jefferson and Virginia representative James Madison, opposed the idea because their home state of Virginia had nearly paid off its indemnities and because they thought such a measure would put too much power in the hands of the federal government. The Southerners eventually relented on the question in return for Hamilton and his allies' allowing the federal capital to be moved from New York to a

Once Hamilton reached the presidential cabinet, he used those newly enumerated powers to almost single-handedly forge a partnership between the public sector and private banks that would bind the country together and attract the capital to power the young nation's economy.

new district on the Potomac River. Jefferson and Madison would not be so agreeable in the future, though, and the charter of the First National Bank of the United States in 1791 was the the highwater mark of Hamilton's power and influence.

The bank's ownership would be split between private investors and the Treasury Department at a ratio of 4 to 1, with the federal government maintaining the right to oversee the bank's books. The bank was massive for its time: its $10 million in initial capital (roughly $260 million in 2015 dollars) was more than three times as large as the combined capital of the five state-chartered banks. Its large size enabled it to market federal debt across the country and abroad, leading to low and stable interest rates and a sound currency.

In conceiving of the bank, Hamilton drew heavily on the lessons he learned during his childhood on St. Croix and his experiences during the war. Both the pre-war West Indian economy and

that of the American Revolution suffered from a lack of overall money and a dearth of confidence in what currency was available. With the debts of the states now assumed by the federal government, he set out to establish a bank that would be financed by the private sector and would in turn finance the federal government. Government bonds, bought and sold by the bank, solved this liquidity problem and served as a sound currency that was backed by the full faith and credit of the United States.

The battles that Jefferson and Hamilton fought 250 years ago, in other words, are still being waged today.

WATCHING THE WATCHMEN *The legacy of Hamilton, left, looms large over today's Treasury; above, distrust of federal banking oversight enflamed Occupy Wall Street protesters in 2011.*

The bank's effects weren't all positive, however. The creation of the bank flooded the economy with new money, and the marketing of bank stock and government debt helped trigger the first speculative fever and financial panic of the nation's history. After the bubble burst, Hamilton was able to dampen the effects of the crisis by stepping into the Treasury market with federal funds to buy government debt and assuage the markets. But the episode showed the downside of Hamiltonian capitalism: it empowered unscrupulous financiers to manipulate the credit system for their own gain, regardless of the consequences for the public good.

Though central banking has evolved since Hamilton's time, the basic framework that he created—a largely private banking system with public oversight—remains to this day. The commingling of public and private purpose can have a huge stimulative effect on the economy but, as demonstrated in the 2008 financial crisis, it can also lead to abuses. The battles that Jefferson and Hamilton fought 250 years ago, in other words, are still being waged today.

Christopher Matthews, a writer at Fortune, *covers economics, real estate and financial markets.*

A MAN OF MANY WORDS: THE LETTERS OF ALEXANDER HAMILTON

Who knows what great men were really thinking? We do when they are as eager to put quill to paper as this Founding Father

BY DANIEL S. LEVY

ALEXANDER HAMILTON WAS AN ALMOST OBSESSIVE WRITER. His work ranges from political tracts penned as a student at King's College to critical military letters delivered on behalf of Gen. George Washington during his time as an aide-de-camp to notes sent to various associates that parsed local and national politics. And then, of course, there is the personal correspondence to family and friends. Taken together, the more than 6,000 letters available on the National Archives Founders Online site *founders.archives.gov* chart not only his life but the tumultuous birth of the United States, including Hamilton's many contributions to its form and direction. The following smattering of the man's vast output touches on his troubled lineage, his search for love and his frustrations with war. Through it all, his vision for America, not to mention his enmity toward Aaron Burr, comes at the reader loud and clear. The excerpts, which are reprinted with Hamilton's abbreviations and misspellings intact, reveal a man of the Enlightenment whose thoughts transcend his time.

ON ENCOURAGING WASHINGTON TO RUN FOR PRESIDENT

Hamilton had previously urged his old commander to accept the presidency, suggesting in a letter in September 1788 that the "necessity of your filling the station in question is so universal." His once and future boss was flattered by Hamilton's "frankness" and how he had "dealt thus freely and like a friend." In the letter of Nov. 18, 1788, at right, Hamilton continued to push, saying that "no other man can sufficiently unite the public opinion or can give the requisite weight to the office in the commencement of the Government." Further, Washington's refusal to accept "would have the worst effect imaginable." The rest is American history.

May this be printed?

MSS. Vol. 4, p. 49 (17)

p 199

Hamilton to Washington.

November 18, 1788.

Dear Sir.

+

* * * * *

Your last letter on a certain subject I have received. I feel a conviction that you will finally see your acceptance to be indispensable. It is no compliment to say that no other man can sufficiently unite the public opinion, nor can give the requisite weight to the office in the commencement of the government. These considerations appear to me of themselves decisive. I am not sure that your refusal would not throw everything into confusion. I am sure that it would have the worst effect imaginable. Indeed, as I hinted in a former letter, I think circumstances leave no option.

I remain,
Dear Sir,
Your affectionate and
humble servant
A. Hamilton.

His Excellency Genl. Washington.

+ These stars and those at the commencement of the [illegible]

On Recruiting Slaves for the Revolution

March 14, 1779, to John Jay

John Jay

Hamilton had abhorred slavery since witnessing its brutality as a child in the Caribbean. Four years into the American Revolution, he suggested to Jay, president of the Continental Congress, that slaves be allowed to enlist in the fight against the British. And he recommended they be granted their freedom in return for their service.

"I mention this, because I frequently hear it objected to the scheme of embodying negroes that they are too stupid to make soldiers. This is so far from appearing to me a valid objection that I think their want of cultivation (for their natural faculties are probably as good as ours) joined to that habit of subordination which they acquire from a life of servitude, will make them sooner became soldiers than our White inhabitants. Let officers be men of sense and sentiment, and the nearer the soldiers approach to machines perhaps the better.

"I foresee that this project will have to combat much opposition from prejudice and self-interest. The contempt we have been taught to entertain for the blacks, makes us fancy many things that are founded neither in reason nor experience; and an unwillingness to part with property of so valuable a kind will furnish a thousand arguments to show the impracticability or pernicious tendency of a scheme which requires such a sacrifice.... An essential part of the plan is to give them their freedom with their muskets. This will secure their fidelity, animate their courage, and I believe will have a good influence upon those who remain, by opening a door to their emancipation."

On the Search for a Wife

April 1779, to Lt. Col. John Laurens

John Laurens

Laurens, who joined Gen. Washington's staff in 1777, eventually became Hamilton's closest friend. In the spring of 1779, he was headed to South Carolina, and the 24-year-old Hamilton asked that Laurens find him a mate while he was down there. His wish list of required attributes was impressively long.

"And Now my Dear as we are upon the subject of wife, I empower and command you to get me one in Carolina.... She must be young, handsome (I lay most stress upon a good shape), sensible (a little learning will do), well bred (but she must have an aversion to the word *ton*), chaste and tender (I am an enthusiast in my notions of fidelity and fondness) of some good nature, a great deal of generosity (she must neither love money nor scolding, for I dislike equally a termagent and an œconomist). In politics, I am indifferent what side she may be of; I think I have arguments that will easily convert her to mine. As to religion a moderate stock will satisfy me. She must believe in god and hate a saint. But as to fortune, the larger stock of that the better.... If you should not readily meet with a lady that you think answers my description you can only advertise in the public papers.... To excite their emulation, it will be necessary for you to give an account of the lover—his size, make, quality of mind and body, achievements, expectations, fortune, &c. In drawing my picture, you will no doubt be civil to your friend; mind you do justice to the length of my nose."

On the Misery of War

Sept. 12, 1780, to Laurens

By the late summer of 1780, the Continental Army had been fighting the British for five long years. Hamilton, clearly worn down by the rigors of the campaign, needed to vent to someone about the unending struggle and its unyielding hardships.

"You can hardly conceive in how dreadful a situation we are. The army, in the course of the present month, has received only four or five days rations of meal, and we really know not of any adequate relief in future. This distress at such a stage of the campaign sours the soldiery. 'Tis in vain you make apologies to them. The officers are out of humour, and the worst of evils seems to be coming upon us—a loss of our virtue.... The truth is I am an unlucky honest man, that speak my sentiments to all and with emphasis. I say this to you because you know it and will not charge me with vanity. I hate Congress—I hate the army—I hate the world—I hate myself. The whole is a mass of fools and knaves."

On the Ratification Debate

October 1787, to George Washington

George Washington

Once delegates in Philadelphia created a new constitution, it had to be ratified by the states. Hamilton took the opportunity to inform his former commander of what he expected to be an arduous process—and sent a copy of a piece he wrote attacking anti-Federalist New York governor George Clinton.

"The New Constitution is as popular in this City as it is possible for any thing to be—and the prospect thus far is favourable to it throughout the state. But there is no saying what turn things may take when the full flood of official influence is let loose against it. This is to be expected, for though the Governor has not publicly declared himself his particular connections and confidential friends are loud against it."

On His Distrust of Aaron Burr

Sept. 21, 1792, to an unknown recipient

Aaron Burr

In 1789 Hamilton's father-in-law, Gen. Philip Schuyler, became one of New York's first two senators. But when Schuyler, a Federalist, ran for re-election, anti-Federalist opponents nominated Burr to replace him. When Burr's campaign succeeded, it made a lifelong enemy of Hamilton. Here, he makes his feelings toward Burr abundantly clear.

"I fear the other Gentleman [Burr] is unprincipled both as a public and private man. When the constitution was in deliberation, his conduct was equivocal; but its enemies, who I believe best understood him considered him as with them. In fact, I take it, he is for or against nothing, but as it suits his interest or ambition. He is determined, as I conceive, to make his way to be the head of the popular party and to climb per *fas et nefas* to the highest honors of the state; and as much higher as circumstances may permit. Embarrassed, as I understand, in his circumstances, with an extravagant family—bold enterprising and intriguing, I am mistaken, if it be not his object to play the game of confusion, and I feel it a religious duty to oppose his career."

On the Affair

July 1797, in a pamphlet

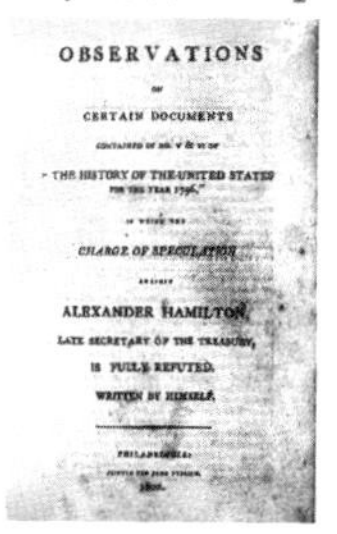

OBSERVATIONS

CERTAIN DOCUMENTS

"THE HISTORY OF THE UNITED STATES

CHARGE OF SPECULATION

ALEXANDER HAMILTON,

LATE SECRETARY OF THE TREASURY,

IS FULLY REFUTED.

WRITTEN BY HIMSELF.

In "Observations on Certain Documents Contained in No. V & VI of 'The History of the United States for the Year 1796,' In Which the Charge of Speculation Against Alexander Hamilton, Late Secretary of the Treasury, is Fully Refuted. Written by Himself," Hamilton sought to get out ahead of the damage brought on by revelations of his affair with Maria Reynolds. By responding so forthrightly to accusations not only about the relationship but also of financial wrongdoing, he hoped to show he had nothing to hide. An implication that Maria and her husband had planned the entanglement as a blackmail ploy from the beginning couldn't have hurt.

"The charge against me is a connection with one James Reynolds for purposes of improper pecuniary speculation. My real crime is an amorous connection with his wife, for a considerable time with his privity and connivance, if not originally brought on by a combination between the husband and wife with the design to extort money from me.

"This confession is not made without a blush. I cannot be the apologist of any vice because the ardour of passion may have made it mine. I can never cease to condemn myself for the pang, which it may inflict in a bosom eminently intitled to all my gratitude, fidelity and love. But that bosom will approve, that even at so great an expence, I should effectually wipe away a more serious stain from a name, which it cherishes with no less elevation than tenderness. The public too will I trust excuse the confession. The necessity of it to my defence against a more heinous charge could alone have extorted from me so painful an indecorum."

On His Past

Aug. 26, 1800, to William Jackson

William Jackson

Hamilton and Jackson were old friends, having worked together on Washington's staff during the war. Jackson and Laurens went to Paris in 1781 to see about getting a loan and supplies from France, and at the Constitutional Conven-

tion, Jackson served as secretary of the meeting. He and Hamilton were so close that Hamilton entrusted Jackson with information about his affair with Maria Reynolds, and here with "the real history" of his ancestry and birth. It was a topic that still clearly pained him as an adult.

"Never was there a more ungenerous persecution of any man than of myself.—Not only the worst constructions are put upon my conduct as a public man but it seems my birth is the subject of the most humiliating criticism. . . . I think it proper to confide to your bosom the real history of it, that among my friends you may if you please wipe off some part of the stain which is so industriously impressed. . . .

"My Grandfather by the mothers side of the name of Faucette was a French Huguenot who emigrated to the West Indies in consequence of the revocation of the Edict of Nantz and settled in the Island of Nevis and there acquired a pretty fortune. I have been assured by persons who knew him that he was a man of letters and much of a gentleman. He practiced a[s] a Physician, whether that was his original profession, or one assumed for livelihood after his emigration is not to me ascertained.

"My father now dead was certainly of a respectable Scotch Fami[ly.] His father was, and the son of his Eldest brother now is Laird of Grang[e.] His mother was the sister of an ancient Baronet Sir Robert Pollock. . . . For some time he was supported by his friends in Scotland, and for several years before his death by me. It was his ault to have had too much pride and too large a portion of indolence—but his character was otherwise without reproach and his manners those of a Gentleman."

On Choosing Jefferson over Burr for President

Dec. 16, 1800, to Oliver Wolcott Jr.

At first, presidential elections were not decided by popular vote but rather by electors appointed by each state's legislature. The candidate with the most votes became president, and the runner-up was vice president. In 1800, Burr and Thomas Jefferson tied with 73 votes each, sending the decision to the House of Representatives, where

Oliver Wolcott Jr.

it resulted in 35 more deadlocks. While Hamilton opposed Jefferson's ideas, he disliked Burr even more. He lobbied many influencers, including Wolcott—his successor as secretary of the Treasury—to ensure that Burr would be denied. On the 36th vote, Jefferson and Hamilton got what they wanted.

"There is no doubt but that upon every virtuous and prudent calculation Jefferson is to be preferred. He is by far not so dangerous a man and he has pretensions to character.

"As to Burr there is nothing in his favour. His private character is not defended by his most partial friends. He is bankrupt beyond redemption except by the plunder of his country. His public principles have no other spring or aim than his own aggrandizement."

On His Son's Death

Feb. 29, 1802, to Gouverneur Morris

Gouverneur Morris

In late 1801, George Eacker gave a speech against Hamilton, and Hamilton's eldest son, Philip, and a friend, Richard Price, taunted the lawyer about it. Eacker branded the men "a set of rascals," and two duels were set. On November 22, Price and Eacker faced off in Paulus Hook, N.J. Neither was hit. The next day it was Hamilton's turn. This time, Eacker's bullet struck its target, above the hip. The 19-year-old died the following day. The passing of his son devastated Hamilton and the family. Months later, Morris, at the time serving in the U.S. Senate, received word of his friend's profoundly unsettled state.

"Mine is an odd destiny. Perhaps no man in the UStates has sacrificed or done more for the present Constitution than myself—and contrary to all my anticipations of its fate, as you know from the very begginning I am still labouring to prop the frail and worthless fabric. Yet I have the murmurs of its friends no less than the curses of its foes for my rewards. What can I do better than withdraw from the Scene? Every day proves to me more and more that this American world was not made for me."

INK STAINED *Hamilton churned out many of his writings on this lap desk, housed at the Grange, his recently restored home in northern Manhattan.*

On His Own Death

July 4, 1804, to Elizabeth Hamilton

Elizabeth Hamilton

Both Hamilton and Burr kept their upcoming duel a secret from their families. Still, each prepared letters in the event they were killed. Burr wrote to his beloved daughter Theodosia Burr Alston: "I am indebted to you, my dearest Theodosia, for a very great portion of the happiness which I have enjoyed in this life. You have completely satisfied all that my heart and affections had hoped or even wished. . . . Adieu. Adieu." Hamilton penned a similar farewell to his wife. He died the following week.

"This letter, my very dear Eliza, will not be delivered to you, unless I shall first have terminated my earthly career; to begin, as I humbly hope from redeeming grace and divine mercy, a happy immortality.

"If it had been possible for me to have avoided the interview, my love for you and my precious children would have been alone a decisive motive. But it was not possible, without sacrifices which would have rendered me unworthy of your esteem. I need not tell you of the pangs I feel, from the idea of quitting you and exposing you to the anguish which I know you would feel. Nor could I dwell on the topic lest it should unman me.

"The consolations of Religion, my beloved, can alone support you; and these you have a right to enjoy. Fly to the bosom of your God and be comforted. With my last idea; I shall cherish the sweet hope of meeting you in a better world.

"Adieu best of wives and best of Women. Embrace all my darling Children for me."

A CITY MANSE FOR AN URBANE FOUNDER

The Grange, Hamilton's house on a hill, was the only home he ever owned. After he died, though, it became more of a mobile home

BY COURTNEY MIFSUD

THE CHARMING PALE YELLOW HOUSE sits unassumingly on a hillside corner of St. Nicholas Park in the West Harlem neighborhood of Manhattan. A passerby would be forgiven for missing the small plaque on the low black fence along its walk, the one that reads THE GRANGE: HOME OF ALEXANDER HAMILTON. Other Founding Fathers left behind loud architectural legacies. George Washington had his Mount Vernon; Thomas Jefferson his Monticello. But if Hamilton was more outgoing than his Revolutionary contemporaries, his homestead was considerably more understated than either of theirs.

To be sure, Hamilton was born of different stock. In his family, there was no estate to pass along. It likely would not have mattered in any case. Hamilton always seemed destined to settle not on any of the Caribbean islands of his youth but rather in one of the mainland's bustling cities.

Yet, though you might expect he'd be eager to quickly put down roots, to find something permanent after a peripatetic early life, he in fact spent his first 29 years in New York moving still more—from house to house in Lower Manhattan, owning none of them. It wasn't until the late 1790s, his career in public service mostly through, that Hamilton decided to build a tranquil retreat.

He undertook what he called his "sweet project" despite ongoing financial troubles. Being a Founding Father did not pay particularly well, and too proud to accept money from his in-laws, Hamilton had stretched his credit to the limit. But while renting a small house in Harlem Heights, in what was essentially the countryside of northern Manhattan, he found the best plot he could plausibly afford: 15 acres, perched high enough on a hill to offer views of Manhattan's two bordering rivers. He was so taken by the spot that he soon bought 20 acres more. But the property, though picturesque, was not quite perfect: from there, it was an hour-and-a-half commute by carriage to his law offices at the other end of the island.

Hamilton chose John McComb Jr. to design his dream house. McComb, a seasoned architect, had built Gracie Mansion and would later design New York's City Hall, but Hamilton knew him because as one of his first acts as Treasury secretary he had commissioned McComb to build a lighthouse for

OPEN HOUSE *A restored Hamilton Grange National Memorial, above, welcomes the public not far from where it originally stood. Below: The Grange at its first address*

RELOCATED *For almost 120 years, the Grange sat wedged against St. Luke's Church on Convent Avenue.*

Cape Henry in Virginia.

In 1802 the residence was completed in the Federal style, the Romanesque architecture favored by the Founding Fathers for both their homes and government buildings. Hamilton named it the Grange, after both his uncle's St. Croix plantation and his grandfather's estate in Scotland.

The Grange may seem compact when compared with the sprawling Monticello or the colossal Mount Vernon, but for New York City it was grand enough. The two-story building featured not one but two octagonal rooms, one of them a dining room with tall French windows. When the connecting doors to the parlor were open, the combined space provided an expansive and elegant entertaining space. A small study off the foyer featured his bookshelves and held a rolling desk, where Hamilton wrote his letters. Outside, large porches cosseted the front, verandas ran along both sides, and a row of 13 sweet gum trees near the entrance paid homage to the original colonies.

Guests arriving by the front door were greeted by a marble bust of the homeowner portrayed as a Roman senator. Giuseppe Ceracchi, the young sculptor who created it, had made similar likenesses for other luminaries. But Ceracchi was more used-car salesman than artist to the stars. Hamilton was flattered when the artist approached him about producing the bust, and he was happy to sit while Ceracchi molded the terra-cotta cast. But when the sculptor returned with the piece from Florence, where it was recast in white marble, he had another gift as well: an unexpected bill of $620, or $15,000 today. Hamilton was not pleased with the bill, but his family actually liked the bust and pushed him to pay the extortionate price.

It turns out that Ceracchi had pulled the same scam on Washington and Jefferson. The father of our country, in fact, ended up with three busts, which he displayed for a while before returning them; he never paid. Not only did Jefferson buy his bust, though, but he acquired a copy of Hamilton's

MOVING DAY *In 2008 the Grange was lifted off its foundation and rolled around the corner to St. Nicholas Park.*

ROOMS FOR A VIEW *The centerpiece on the table in the dining room, above left, belonged to the Hamiltons, as did the pianoforte, right, a favorite of the children. But the bust of Hamilton, below, is a replica of the infamous Ceracchi original.*

too, putting them both—each facing the other—in Monticello's entrance hall. Later, one of Jefferson's grandchildren would note that the two were "opposed in death as in life."

In the end, Hamilton was able to enjoy the Grange for only two years. After his fatal duel in 1804, his beloved Eliza was left with her husband's debts but not the house, which was sold at auction. But using the inheritance she received after her father's death and some donations from generous friends, she soon bought it back. And she would live at the Grange for nearly three more decades until she sold it before moving to Washington, D.C., in 1833.

Afterward, a stream of renters moved in and out as the property slowly deteriorated. In 1889 the house was set to be demolished to make room for the expanding street grid. Just before the Grange was lost forever, its owner, Amos Cotting, donated it to St. Luke's Episcopal Church. The church was in the process of relocating uptown and needed a temporary chapel until the new one was completed. So the elders brought in a construction firm to lift the Grange off its foundation, and drawn by horses, the house—minus a porch or two—was taken to Convent Avenue, 500 feet away. When the new church was erected, the house was wedged beside it and turned into a rectory.

There the house remained until 1924, when the American Scenic and Historic Preservation Society had the idea to transform it into a Hamilton museum. The society's president cajoled a pair of philanthropists, George F. Baker Sr. and J.P. Morgan Jr., to purchase the house and donate it to the society, which then filled it with period pieces that reflected Hamilton's taste. In 1962, Congress passed legislation that again transferred ownership of the house, again in disrepair, this time to the National Park Foundation and the National Park Service, which promptly renamed it the Hamilton Grange National Memorial. The authorization was contingent on further restoration and another relocation, a plan approved by the New York State Assembly way back in 1908. It took more than 30 years for the National Park Service to come up with a suitable strategy and an additional decade before the restoration was under way. In 2008, Wolfe House and Building Movers of Pennsylvania used computerized hydraulic dollies to move the house one more time, from Convent Avenue to St. Nicholas Park. After two years of work—a remade roof, a rewired electrical system, reappointed era-specific decorative touches—Hamilton Grange opened its doors in 2011. Its present site overlaps the land its first owner once bought.

Today, guided tours visit several rooms furnished in original Grange-era decor. A replica of the Ceracchi bust faces what would have been the front door. In the parlor sits a pianoforte, the real version of the one featured in the current Broadway musical. The study showcases several books that bear Eliza Hamilton's signature.

Other Founding Fathers have national memorials, but only Hamilton's was built by the man it honors.

BURR, THAT'S COLD
Accounts differed as to whether Hamilton even tried to fire before he was laid low.

A "DANGEROUS" MAN LIVES UP TO THE INSULT

Alexander Hamilton always spoke his mind. In the end, it proved his fatal flaw

BY JOHN SEDGWICK

THE MOST FAMOUS DUEL OF ALL TIME seems inevitable now, but that's history for you. It transforms even the most startling turns of events into matters of destiny. You could say Alexander Hamilton and Aaron Burr were bound for their explosive collision simply because they were similar enough in interests and abilities to be drawn together but different enough to be violently opposed once they were. That's mostly true, as far as it goes.

Both men were orphaned at an early age, but while the teenaged Hamilton arrived in New York in 1773 as a penniless immigrant, Burr was a near-aristocrat, the son of the late president of Princeton. Fed by class tensions, their unfriendly competitiveness started almost as soon as Hamilton disembarked in Manhattan, when he decided against attending Princeton because he wouldn't be allowed to graduate as quickly as he heard Burr had. When war came, the ambitious Hamilton again envied Burr's station, in this case his glorious field command; Hamilton was stuck behind a desk in Washington's headquarters. But the equally striving Burr was envious as well, in particular of Hamilton's membership in the General's "family" of assisting officers while Burr himself was risking his life in anonymity.

After the peace of 1783, the pair became the two finest lawyers in New York City, often ending up on opposite sides of cases. And though

Opposed in so many things, Hamilton and Burr were united in the recognition that by 1804 their honor was about all they had left. Their careers largely rested on their reputation, and for each of them, that reputation lay in tatters.

they soon found themselves on opposite sides of the political aisle as well, they might have survived their intertwined lives, but for this: in 1804, after Burr had to settle for the vice presidency, Hamilton came to view his foe as a demagogue, proclaiming him "dangerous." Burr, taking umbrage, decided to settle things once and for all.

The notion of a duel—from *duellum*, a contraction of *duo bellum*, or "war of two"—descended from medieval contests of rivalrous knights. By the time the duel migrated to America, the traditional weapons of chivalry had been exchanged for pistols, often quite handsome ones—engraved, hand finished, and long-barreled for greater accuracy—that were frequently kept as a pair in a velvet-lined mahogany case. And the animating sentiment had fluffed out into a grander sort of masculine pride that wasn't intended to impress the courts, women or the Crown but to awe a small circle of gentlemen who shared their particular notion of personal honor.

Opposed in so many things, Hamilton and Burr were united in the recognition that by 1804 their honor was about all they had left. Their careers largely rested on their reputation, and for each of them, that reputation lay in tatters. For both, tales of sexual transgressions were the fundamental indignities, but their financial affairs were also in ruin, and they had been largely discarded by political parties they had either created or transformed. Once serene or haughty in the face of attack, both men had grown twitchy, hypersensitive to slights that they might once have brushed off.

Yet if they agreed on the value of honor, the two disagreed about the necessity of killing to defend it. Having sacrificed a son to the practice, Hamilton was bound to consider the ritual "abhorrent," even though he had participated in it countless times. Hamilton was involved in 11 duels, most of them toward the end of his life, but only the last involved potentially lethal gunfire. Burr was involved in only two, both against members of the Hamilton family, and both required pistols to resolve.

Hamilton had called Burr a "dangerous" man in late winter. Shortly afterward, though, in one of the strange twists that were forever conjoining the two, Burr had ridden through the snowdrifts for several hours by moonlight from Richmond Hill up to the Grange, Hamilton's country seat high above the Hudson. Hamilton was not entirely surprised to see the somewhat haggard peer before him. Burr was in need of "immediate pecuniary assistance"—$10,000, to save his house. But Hamilton did not snicker, as he might have. Instead, he turned to his brother-in-law, who—despite his own nearly lethal run-in with Burr—agreed to float Burr a loan.

But that was then.

IN THE TWO-WEEK PERIOD FROM the close of the negotiations on June 27 to the duel on July 11, Hamilton and Burr carried on with their lives as though everything were normal. Hamilton continued to live in his law office downtown, venturing to the Grange for only a few days at a time. He never told his wife of the duel, sure that she would forbid it. Just a week before, Hamilton hosted a ball for 75, including the artist John Trumbull, who had done his full-size portrait, and, in the warm weather, Hamilton had encouraged the guests to spill out to the garden and the wood beyond, where musicians hid among the trees. A widower, Burr spent most evenings at Richmond Hill, some of the evenings shivering in front of a fire, even in July. But Hamilton and Burr both passed the evening of July Fourth at the Society of the Cincinnati, a club for old soldiers of the Revolutionary War, of which Hamilton was president and Burr a member. Everyone noticed that the two men were not their normal selves, but no one knew the cause. Trumbull was there, and he noticed that "contrary to his wont," Burr "was silent, gloomy, sour." Hamilton, in contrast, "entered with glee into the gaiety of a convivial dinner party." The evening called for drinking songs, and both men obliged, Hamilton actually climbing onto a table to deliver his in a pleasant tenor, while Burr gazed up at him, rapt.

Why, soldiers, why
Should we be melancholy, boys? Why, soldiers, why?
Whose business 'tis to die? What! Sighing? Fie!
Damn fear, drink on, be jolly boys!
'Tis he, you, or I.

It was up to Hamilton to select the pistols, since he was the challenged party, and he chose the very pair his son had used. Made by Wogdon, the London gunsmith, they were owned by Hamilton's brother-in-law John Barker Church. Flintlock pistols, they were heavy, each one weighing

HEAVY METAL *The flintlock pistols of John Barker Church served neither his brother-in-law nor his nephew well.*

several pounds, and featured dark-walnut stocks and handsome brass barrels of menacing length. They were not weapons for the unpracticed.

That last night before the duel, Hamilton had been up late at his town house on Cedar Street, completing his will, creating a rather grim financial accounting of his estate, tidying up other affairs, and writing a last round of letters to friends. And he stole some time to write an explanation of his conduct in the run-up to the duel, one that, as he may have known, would shape the campaign to secure his reputation in the case of his death. He insisted he would "throw away" his "first fire" and possibly his second—the same tactic he had recommended to his son—the better to encourage Burr to "pause and reflect." Before firing, presumably. Since this had led to the death of his son, it is surprising that Hamilton would think of it this time. More, it hints at a fatalism that verges on the suicidal, as Hamilton planned to stand defenseless before Burr, leaving it to his worst enemy to shoot him dead.

He finished with a note to his wife, which was to be delivered to her only in the case of his death. Up at the Grange, she had no idea of her husband's plans. An orphaned boy was staying with him, and late that night, Hamilton found him reading a book in Hamilton's study. Hamilton laid his hands on top of the boy's and recited the Lord's Prayer; then he settled back in a chair, and the child soon fell asleep in Hamilton's arms. Roaming the house, he woke his son John, who was with him, to tell him he would be going later to the Grange so the boy wouldn't worry to find him gone in the morning. Finally he returned to his own bed.

Hamilton rose before dawn and arrived first at the Manhattan docks. From there four oarsmen rowed him across the Hudson, with a friend, Nathaniel Pendleton, who would serve as his second, and Dr. David Hosack, who had attended to his dying son, Philip. Hamilton had wanted him along; Burr professed not to see the point of having a doctor present.

Burr had passed the night at Richmond Hill, much of it writing a long, chatty letter to his daughter Theodosia, always his favorite correspondent, that said nothing of the duel. Instead, he informed her husband, asking him to keep up her academic studies if he didn't survive. He waited out the days until the duel with increasing impatience. "From 7 to 12 is the least pleasant [time]," he told William Peter Van Ness, his legal minion who was making the arrangements. "Anything so we but get on." But when, on the fateful morning, Van Ness came to walk with Burr down the hill to the dock, he found Burr sound asleep on the couch in front of the fire.

THE SUN WAS JUST DAWNING when the men reached the bluff at Weehawken, and the seconds set about to clear away some brush that had gathered on the dueling ground. They were the ones to pace off the distance and to throw the lot to determine whose second would shout, "Present!," the signal to fire. That fell to Hamilton's man. With no other preliminaries, the two men took their positions across from each other. In the rosy light, at that distance, each could get a good look at the other, to check for a tightening of the eyes or a flickering of the cheek that might betray the obvious tension of the moment. By the code, calmness in the face of annihilation was essential, even as they stood across from each other, in a classic fencer's pose, right foot forward, body sideways, right shoulder up high over the chin. The better, that way, to narrow the profile and protect the vitals from a one-ounce ball of lead that would strike like a tiny cannonball at this distance. Both men wore heavy topcoats to obscure the contours of their bodies. Standing so close, with an index finger curled around the trigger of his pistol, each could scrutinize the other's face—one by now nearly as

IN MEMORIAM *A plaque at 82 Jane Street in Manhattan's West Village marks Hamilton's death, though it actually occurred nearby.*

familiar as his own—for gratifying hints of distress.

It had to have been a singularly terrifying moment, but neither man is said to have betrayed any emotion as he stared the other one down. Finally, Hamilton's second cried out, "Present!"

Each leveled his pistol at the other, and two blasts sounded, with puffs of smoke, in close succession. Burr's ball caught Hamilton on his right side. He gave out a cry of pain as the impact of the bullet twisted him onto the balls of his feet and then sent him sprawling back onto the ground. He lay there stunned, ashen-faced, gasping. Burr took a step toward his fallen enemy, a flash of "regret" on his face, said his second, before he hurriedly left the field without a backward glance.

"I am a dead man," Hamilton told his own second, Pendleton, and added to Hosack, who rushed to his aid, "This is a mortal wound."

And so it was. The bullet had cracked through his ribs, shredded his lungs and pierced his liver before lodging tight against his lower spine, leaving him paralyzed all down his legs as blood pooled in his gut. Pendleton and Hosack eased him down the steep slope and into the rowboat, which conveyed him back to Manhattan, every stroke of the oars excruciating.

The news from Weehawken went up as a bulletin at the Tontine coffeehouse, a gathering spot for the city's business class. *General Hamilton was shot by Colonel Burr this morning in a duel, the general is said to be mortally wounded.* The electrifying news spread quickly in every direction, and an eerie quiet settled over much of the island. Much of the city's business stopped, and on the street, people were desperate to find out what others had heard.

Despite his agony, as he lay on his deathbed at a friend's house in Manhattan, Hamilton tried to comfort his delicate wife, who had rushed to his side from the Grange, thunderstruck at the news. She'd dissolved into a fit of explosive weeping the moment she saw him. "Remember, my Eliza, you are a Christian," Hamilton urged her. To soothe

Who Shot First?

According to the two eyewitnesses at the duel, the shots were not fired simultaneously, but rather about four or five seconds apart. It is an unusual gap. Aside from separating the calm from the impatient, the delay suggests a divergence in strategy that says something about the otherwise mysterious mind-sets of the two men. Who shot first? Was it Burr, the more soldierly one, firing immediately to deliver a mortal wound? Or was it Hamilton, immediately "throwing away" his fire, as he had claimed he would—and then leaving it to Burr to shoot him at his leisure if he chose?

The Hamilton forces insisted that it was Burr and that Hamilton's gun had gone off only by a spastic reflex. Hamilton's second, Nathaniel Pendleton, returned to the dueling ground the next day and claimed to find a cherry-tree branch "about 12 and a half feet" up from where Hamilton stood that seemed to have been drilled by his bullet.

REVENGE *Hamilton lost the battle but afterward won the war of public opinion.*

The Burr camp maintained that it was Hamilton and that their man had no way of knowing his adversary hadn't shot to kill. "The falsehood 'that H. fired only when falling & without aim' has given to very improper suggestions . . . ," Burr later wrote in an unusually clipped style that revealed his anxiety about the matter. To show that Hamilton fully intended to shoot with purpose, the Burr camp contributed the detail that after the distance had been paced off, and with the two men facing each other down, Hamilton stopped the proceedings to say the sunlight was glinting off his glasses, obscuring his vision. John McLane Hamilton, however, said his grandfather didn't wear glasses.

Burr was determined to show that he had followed the prescriptions of the *code duello*; the Hamilton people contended that Burr had killed a defenseless man in cold blood. If the evidence favors the former, it has been the latter position that has won the day. In this, the dead Hamilton outdid the living Burr.

herself, she fanned him throughout the rest of the hot day. Her beguiling sister Angelica came and crumpled into tears too.

Hamilton sought Communion, but neither minister he summoned would oblige a man dying from a duel. "I have no ill will against Colonel Burr," he assured the second one, the Episcopal bishop Benjamin Moore. "I met him with a fixed resolution to do him no harm. I forgive all that happened." With that, Bishop Moore gave Hamilton the sacrament after all. He labored through the night, and in the morning Eliza brought in his seven children and stood them at the foot of his bed, a sight that left Hamilton unable to speak. More friends came, 20 in all, a scene of desperate grief. Only Hamilton, it appeared, was able to keep his composure. His last words were political: "If they break this union, they will break my heart." He died so easily, his wife weeping beside him, that people did not immediately realize he was gone.

Afterward, Eliza opened the letter that he'd written her in the event of his death. He concluded stirringly:

Fly to the bosom of your God
and be comforted.
With my last idea, I shall cherish
the sweet hope of meeting you in a
better world.
Adieu best of wives and best of
women.
Embrace all my darling children
for me.

Newspapers of every political slant were filled with the story of the death, the ones favoring Hamilton's Federalist Party framing their accounts with borders of funereal black. The city was consumed with grief. "The feelings of the whole community are agonized beyond description," wrote one New Yorker, who added that there was a greater outpouring for Hamilton than there had been even for Washington upon his death five years before.

A state funeral was staged two days later. While massive guns boomed along the Battery and church bells rang sorrowfully all about the city, the New York militia marched through the city in formation, their muzzles pointed downward in memory and respect, leading Hamilton's mahogany casket east along Beekman, down Pearl, past Whitehall and to Broadway, carving a line around what would be the financial center of the world that Hamilton had largely created. The casket was borne by eight pallbearers, with Hamilton's wife and children trailing behind, and then Hamilton's riderless horse, the boots reversed in the stirrups. At Trinity Church, the mourners packed the pews to hear a stirring eulogy by the stylish Gouverneur Morris, the longtime friend of Hamilton who had also given the eulogy for Washington, and from there the mourning spread throughout the country, declaimed in pulpits and retailed in newspapers, until it seemed that everyone knew that Alexander Hamilton had been murdered by Aaron Burr.

Fought to secure Burr's reputation, the duel ended up ruining it, as political spinners of the day succeeded in portraying him as a killer. While Hamilton's reputa-

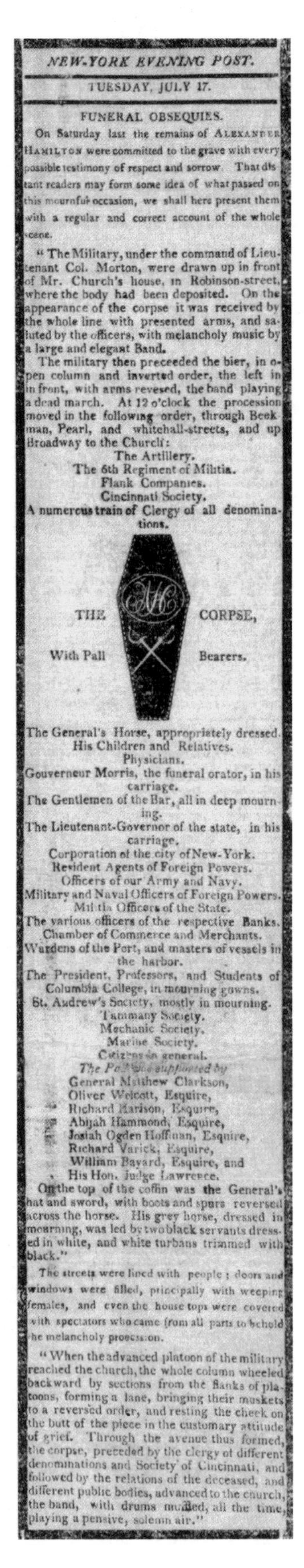

NEW-YORK EVENING POST.

TUESDAY, JULY 17.

FUNERAL OBSEQUIES.

On Saturday last the remains of ALEXANDER HAMILTON were committed to the grave with every possible testimony of respect and sorrow. That distant readers may form some idea of what passed on this mournful occasion, we shall here present them with a regular and correct account of the whole scene.

"The Military, under the command of Lieutenant Col. Morton, were drawn up in front of Mr. Church's house, in Robinson-street, where the body had been deposited. On the appearance of the corpse it was received by the whole line with presented arms, and saluted by the officers, with melancholy music by a large and elegant Band.

The military then preceeded the bier, in open column and inverted order, the left in in front, with arms revesed, the band playing a dead march. At 12 o'clock the procession moved in the following order, through Beekman, Pearl, and whitehall-streets, and up Broadway to the Church:

The Artillery.
The 6th Regiment of Militia.
Flank Companies.
Cincinnati Society.
A numerous train of Clergy of all denominations.

THE CORPSE,
With Pall Bearers.

The General's Horse, appropriately dressed.
His Children and Relatives.
Physicians.
Gouverneur Morris, the funeral orator, in his carriage.
The Gentlemen of the Bar, all in deep mourning.
The Lieutenant-Governor of the state, in his carriage.
Corporation of the city of New-York.
Resident Agents of Foreign Powers.
Officers of our Army and Navy.
Military and Naval Officers of Foreign Powers.
Militia Officers of the State.
The various officers of the respective Banks.
Chamber of Commerce and Merchants.
Wardens of the Port, and masters of vessels in the harbor.
The President, Professors, and Students of Columbia College, in mourning gowns.
St. Andrew's Society, mostly in mourning.
Tammany Society.
Mechanic Society.
Marine Society.
Citizens in general.

The Pa[illegible] supported by
General Matthew Clarkson,
Oliver Wolcott, Esquire,
Richard Harison, Esquire,
Abijah Hammond, Esquire,
Josiah Ogden Hoffman, Esquire,
Richard Varick, Esquire,
William Bayard, Esquire, and
His Hon. Judge Lawrence.

On the top of the coffin was the General's hat and sword, with boots and spurs reversed across the horse. His grey horse, dressed in mourning, was led by two black servants dressed in white, and white turbans trimmed with black."

The streets were lined with people; doors and windows were filled, principally with weeping females, and even the house tops were covered with spectators who came from all parts to behold the melancholy procession.

"When the advanced platoon of the military reached the church, the whole column wheeled backward by sections from the flanks of platoons, forming a lane, bringing their muskets to a reversed order, and resting the cheek on the butt of the piece in the customary attitude of grief. Through the avenue thus formed, the corpse, preceded by the clergy of different denominations and Society of Cincinnati, and followed by the relations of the deceased, and different public bodies, advanced to the church, the band, with drums muffled, all the time, playing a pensive, solemn air."

FUNERAL OBSEQUIES *The* New-York Evening Post *ran this obituary on July 17, 1804.*

SPECTRAL PRESENCE *A bust of Hamilton sits near the spot in Weehawken, N.J., where he was fatally wounded.*

tion soared to a height in death that it had never achieved in life, Burr's dropped to a level unimaginable for a sitting vice president. He slunk out of New York under cover of darkness and traveled south to Georgia incognito. Though a fugitive from justice, he soon returned to Washington to preside over the impeachment trial of Supreme Court Justice Samuel Chase. (He found Chase innocent, much to the irritation of President Thomas Jefferson, who was eager to oust Chase for political reasons.)

Burr went on to engage in what was essentially an act of secession: an attempt to detach the western lands of the Louisiana Purchase from the United States to create a private empire. The scheme collapsed when his co-conspirator, General James Wilkinson, the country's highest-ranking officer, betrayed him to Jefferson. Angered by the Chase decision, not to mention countless other irritations, Jefferson had his former vice president charged with treason. But relevant evidence was not forthcoming, and Burr escaped the gallows.

A year later he fled again, this time to Europe. Hoping to raise funds to revive his conspiracy, he found no backers. By the time he was able to scrounge the fare and the visas to come home, after four years, Burr had nearly starved to death. Shortly after his return, he learned his beloved grandson had died of a fever, and soon after that, his treasured daughter Theodosia drowned in a shipwreck. It was all too much for Burr. Though he lived to be 80, his remaining time was empty. In 1836, he died alone in a cheap hotel on Staten Island and was buried near his father at Princeton, in an unmarked grave.

A RUINED MAN *Though Burr was never tried on murder charges, the duel cast a pall over the rest of his life.*

THE GOOD WIFE: KEEPING A LEGACY ALIVE

Alexander was not always the most loyal husband. Still, Eliza loved and respected him to the end—and for a long time after that

BY RON CHERNOW

FOR ELIZA HAMILTON, THE COLLAPSE OF her world was total, overwhelming and remorseless. Within three years, she had had to cope with four close deaths: her eldest son, her sister Peggy, her mother and her husband, not to mention the mental breakdown of her eldest daughter.

How did Eliza soldier on after these dreadful events that came thick and fast upon her? A month after the duel, she answered a sympathy note from Colonel William S. Smith, who had written to inform her that the Society of the Cincinnati would erect a monument to Hamilton in Trinity Church. In her letter, Eliza alluded to the forces that would sustain her. Suffering from "the irreparable loss of a most amiable and affectionate husband," she prayed for "the mercies of the divine being in whose dispensations" all Christians should acquiesce. Beyond religious solace, she drew strength from sympathetic friends and family members and the veneration paid to her husband. She wrote, "The wounded heart derives a degree of consolation from the tenderness with which its loss is bewailed by the virtuous, the wise, and humane" and "that high honor and respect with which the memory of the dear deceased has been commemorated."

Eliza's fierce, unending loyalty to Hamilton certifies that their marriage had been deeply rewarding, albeit marred by his affair with Maria Reynolds and other misadventures. Blessed with a forgiving heart, Eliza made ample allowance for her husband's flaws. Two months after the duel, she described Hamilton to his friend Nathaniel Pendleton as "my beloved, sainted husband and my guardian angel." She thought that God, in snatching Hamilton away, had balanced the ledgers of her life, inflicting exquisite pain equal to her matchless joy in marriage: "I have remarked to you that I have had a double share of blessings and I must now look forward to grief. . . . For such a husband, his spirit is in heaven and his form in the earth and I am nowhere any part of him is." She pored so frequently over his letters to her that they began to crack and crumble into dust. Around her neck, she wore a tiny bag containing brittle yellow scraps of the love sonnet that Hamilton had given to her during their courtship in Morristown, N.J.—the scraps were sewn together as the paper decomposed—and the intimate farewell let-

MILITANTLY LOYAL *Eliza became a staunch advocate of her husband's legacy and the care of orphaned children.*

ter he had prepared for her on the eve of the duel.

Eliza retained boundless affection for "her Hamilton," even though he had left her stranded in a terrible financial predicament. Hamilton died illiquid if not insolvent. This mocked the hardy Republican fairy tale that he had enriched himself as Treasury secretary and colluded with British paymasters. The secret London bank account that legend said awaited him when the monarchy returned to America—a staple of Jeffersonian lore—had never existed. America's financial wizard earned comparatively little in his lifetime, and his executors feared that any distress sale of his assets—chiefly the Grange and some land in western New York and the Ohio River valley—would slash their value. Gouverneur Morris was appalled by the magnitude of Hamilton's debts and confided to Rufus King:

Our friend Hamilton has been suddenly cut off in the midst of embarrassments which would have required years of professional industry to set straight—a debt of between fifty thousand and sixty thousand dollars hanging over him, a property which in time may sell for seventy or eighty thousand, but which, if brought to the hammer, would not, in all probability, fetch forty.

MEN OF MEANS *With little to inherit from her father, Philip Schuyler, center, Eliza drew upon the kindness of friends of her husband like William S. Smith, left, and Gouverneur Morris, right, to get through the tough period after his death.*

Philip Schuyler had already disposed of a considerable portion of his wealth among his eight children and their descendants—his entire estate of $35,000 could not have covered Hamilton's debts—so Eliza's inheritance fell dreadfully short of Hamilton's more sanguine expectations. She inherited farmland around Albany and Saratoga that yielded a paltry $750 in annual income and did not begin to defray her expenses. Heavily indebted from abortive business ventures, Philip Schuyler died land-rich but cash-poor. The aura of Schuyler family wealth had outdistanced reality.

To keep the family afloat, Gouverneur Morris organized a secret subscription fund among Hamilton's friends. He had to conquer an automatic assumption that the Hamilton children, with their rich grandfather, would never know want. Morris and more than 100 other subscribers poured in about $80,000, while New England Federalists donated Pennsylvania land as well. This fund was such a closely guarded secret that Hamilton's children did not know of it for a generation, and the Bank of New York managed to keep its existence confidential until 1937.

The executors did not dare to dispossess Eliza from the Grange, so they bought it for $30,000 and sold it back to her at half price, ensuring that she could stay there indefinitely. If such generosity preserved Eliza from indigence, it did not spare her incessant anxiety about money and the humiliating need to cadge small loans. Three years after the duel, she appealed to Nathaniel Pendleton for an emergency handout, telling him that "as I am nearly out of cash, I take the liberty to ask you to negotiate a loan of three hundred dollars." Eliza, though never prodigal, had grown up in comfort and now learned to cultivate thrift. Notwithstanding her financial plight, she heeded one sacred injunction in one of Hamilton's farewell letters: to take care of his now blind, poor cousin, Ann Mitchell. Eliza invited her to stay at the Grange for extended periods and bailed her out with a $630 gift in 1810.

Eliza never wavered in her belief that the government owed substantial debts, financial and intangible, to her husband. At the end of the Revolution, Hamilton had waived the pension to which he was entitled as an army officer. From "scruples of delicacy" as a member of Congress, he had sought to eliminate any personal conflict of interest as he pondered the vexed question of veterans' compensation. In a similarly high-minded spirit, he had waived his right to the "bounty" lands awarded to other officers. No amateur when it came to political timing, Eliza bided her time until Thomas Jefferson left the White House in 1809 and then immediately lobbied the apparently more forgiving President James Madison for relief. By the time Madison left office, the persistent Eliza Hamilton had prevailed upon Congress to award her the cash equivalent of 450 acres in bounty lands plus five years' worth of full army pay—about $10,000.

It was a huge struggle for Eliza to educate her children on a modest, fluctuating income. She bemoaned having to raise them in a world of "disastrous events" and "evil passions," but she did a creditable job.

For 10 years after the duel, Eliza clung to the indispensable support of her sister Angelica, her strongest bond to the past and to her fallen husband. A fixture of New York society, Angelica kept busy attending balls and parties until the end. In 1806 her son, Philip, took a large tract of land that he had inherited in upstate New York and established the town of Angelica in her honor. In March 1814, Angelica Church died at 57 and was buried in the same Trinity Churchyard that held the brother-in-law who had so lastingly captivated her. Her husband, John Barker Church, returned to England and died in London in April 1818.

IN HER FIRST DECADES OF widowhood, Eliza had to endure an endless parade of presidents—Jefferson, Madison, James Monroe and John Quincy Adams—who had crossed swords with her husband and had no desire to gild his memory. As "Federalism" became a term of abuse, she embarked on a single-minded crusade to do justice to her husband's achievements. After the Rev. John M. Mason, Timothy Pickering and others failed to produce the major biography that she craved, she turned to her son John Church Hamilton to edit Hamilton's papers and produce a massive history that would duly glorify the patriarch. Eliza buttonholed elderly politicians and peppered them with detailed questionnaires, soliciting their recollections of her husband. She traveled to Mount Vernon and borrowed letters that Hamilton had written to Washington. She knew that she was racing against the clock, against mortality, against the vanishing trove of mementos of the revolutionary years. "I have my fears I shall not obtain my object," she wrote to her daughter Eliza of the seemingly jinxed project in 1832. "Most of the contemporaries of your father have also passed away." The immense biographical project was not completed until seven years after Eliza's death.

The decades that she devoted to conserving her husband's legacy made Eliza only more militantly loyal to his memory, and there was one injury she could never forget: the exposure of the Maria Reynolds affair, for which she squarely blamed James Monroe. In the 1820s, after Monroe had completed two terms as president, he called upon Eliza in Washington, D.C., hoping to thaw the frost between them. Eliza was then about 70 and staying at her daughter's home. She was sitting in the backyard with her 15-year-old nephew when a maid emerged and presented the ex-president's card. Far from being flattered by this distinguished visitor, Eliza was taken aback. "She read the name and stood holding the card, much perturbed," said her nephew. "Her voice sank and she spoke very low, as she always did when she was angry. 'What has that man come to see me for?' " The nephew said that Monroe must have stopped by to pay his respects. She wavered. "I will see him," she finally agreed.

So the small woman with the upright carriage and the sturdy, determined step marched stiffly into the house. When she entered the parlor, Monroe rose to greet her. Eliza then did something out of character and socially unthinkable: she stood facing the ex-president but did not invite him to sit down. With a bow, Monroe began what sounded like a well-rehearsed speech, stating "that it was many years since they had met, that the lapse of time brought its softening influences, that they both were nearing the grave, when past differences could be forgiven and forgotten."

Eliza saw that Monroe was trying to draw a moral equation between them and apportion blame equally for the long rupture in their relationship. Even at this late date, 30 years after the fact, she was not in a forgiving mood. "Mr. Monroe," she told him, "if you have come to tell me that you repent, that you are sorry, very sorry, for the misrepresentations and the slanders and the stories you circulated against my dear husband, if you have come to say this, I understand it. But otherwise, no lapse of time, no nearness to the grave, makes any difference." Monroe took in this rebuke without comment. Stunned by the fiery words delivered by the elderly little woman in widow's weeds, the ex-president picked up his hat, bid Eliza good day and left the house, never to return.

Because Eliza Hamilton tried to erase herself from her husband's story, she has languished in virtually complete historical obscurity. To the extent that she has drawn attention, she has been de-

> *Around her neck, she wore a tiny bag containing brittle yellow scraps of the love sonnet that Hamilton had given to her during their courtship in Morristown.*

GRUDGE AT THE GRANGE *Eliza, above, was not in a forgiving mood toward her husband's nemesis Monroe, below.*

picted as a broken, weeping, neurasthenic creature, clinging to her Bible and lacking any identity other than that of Hamilton's widow. In fact, she was a woman of towering strength and integrity who consecrated much of her extended widowhood to serving widows, orphans and poor children. On March 16, 1806, less than two years after the duel, Eliza and other evangelical women co-founded the New York Orphan Asylum Society, the first private orphanage in New York. Perhaps nothing expressed her affection for Hamilton more tenderly than her efforts on behalf of orphans. If Eliza did not draft the society's constitution, she endorsed its credo that "crime has not been the cause" of the orphan's misery and "future usefulness may yet be the result of [his or her] protection. God himself has marked the fatherless as the peculiar subjects of His divine compassion." Surely some extra dimension of religious fervor had entered into Eliza's feelings toward her husband because of his boyhood. She possessed "her own pitying, loving nature, blended with a rare sense of justice," said her friend Jessie Benton Frémont. "All these she dedicated to the care of orphan children."

FOR MANY YEARS, ELIZA WAS a mainstay of the orphanage board and held the position of second directress, or deputy director. She was present in 1807 when the cornerstone was laid for its two-story wooden headquarters in Greenwich Village. In 1821, Eliza was elevated to first directress with the chief responsibility for the 158 children then housed and educated in the asylum. For the next 27 years, with a tenacity that Hamilton would have savored, she oversaw every aspect of the orphanage work. She raised money, leased properties, visited almshouses, investigated complaints and solicited donations of coal, shoes and Bibles. She often gave the older orphans jobs in her home and helped one gain admittance to West Point. With a finesse reminiscent of her husband's, she handled the society's funds on the finance committee. After obtaining a state charter for the society, she lobbied the state legislature for annual grants. "Mamma, you are a sturdy beggar," her son once teased her. "My dear son," she retorted, "I cannot spare myself or others. My Maker has pointed out this duty to me and has given me the ability and inclination to perform it."

Like her evangelical colleagues, Eliza believed passionately that all children should be literate in order to study the Bible. In 1818 she returned

Monroe took in this rebuke without comment. Stunned by the fiery words delivered by the elderly little woman in widow's weeds, the ex-president picked up his hat, bid Eliza good day and left the house, never to return.

to the state legislature and won a charter for the Hamilton Free School, which was the first educational institution in the Washington Heights section of Manhattan. It stood on land Eliza donated on Broadway between 187th and 188th streets in upper Manhattan and was established in honor of her husband's memory.

A painting of Eliza from later years shows a woman with a strong but kindly face and a firm, determined mouth. Her silver hair was parted down the middle under her widow's cap, and her dark eyes were still large and girlishly bright. "Her face is delicate but full of nerve and spirit. The eyes are very dark and hold the life and energy of the restraining face," said Frémont, who marveled at Eliza's unabated vigor. "When I first lived on the Hudson River, quite near her son's home, it was still remembered how the old lady, past 80, would leave the train at a way station and climb two fences in her shortcut across meadows, rather than go on to the town where the carriage could meet her." Her willpower and spunk surprised people. At one anniversary celebration of the Orphan Asylum Society, Eliza, then in her 90s, materialized, to everyone's amazement—"a very small, upright little figure in deep black, never altered from the time her dark hair was first framed by the widow's cap, until now the hair was white as the cap." Frémont noted how she "retains in an astonishing degree her faculties and converses with much of that ease and brilliancy which lent so peculiar a charm to her younger days."

In 1848 the 91-year-old Eliza moved to Washington, D.C., to live with her younger daughter Eliza, who was now widowed after the death of her husband, Sidney Augustus Holly. At their H Street residence near the White House, Eliza Hamilton cherished her status as a relic of the American Revolution. Like her husband, she was a committed abolitionist who delighted in entertaining slave children from the neighborhood, and she referred derisively to the slaveholding states as the "African States." Always busy knitting or making mats, she was an irresistible curiosity to visitors and a coveted ornament at White House dinners. "Mrs. General Hamilton, upon whom I waited at table, is a very remarkable person," President James K. Polk reported in his diary after one such dinner in February 1846. "She retains her intellect and memory perfectly, and my conversation with her was highly interesting." Eliza aided her friend Dolley Madison in raising money to construct the Washington Monument and remained sharp and alert until the end. When historian Benson J. Lossing interviewed her when she was 91, he found her anything but tearful or morose: "The sunny cheerfulness of her temper and quiet humor . . . still made her deportment genial and attractive."

A devout woman, Eliza never lost her faith that she and Hamilton would be gloriously reunited in the afterlife. She prized a small envelope that Hamilton had once sent her, with a romantic inscription emblazoned across the back: "I heal all wounds but those which love hath made." For Eliza, those wounds had never healed. On Nov. 9, 1854—a turbulent year in which the Kansas-Nebraska Act was enacted and the union that Hamilton had done so much to forge stood gravely threatened—Elizabeth Schuyler Hamilton died at age 97. Her widowhood had lasted 50 years, or slightly longer than her life before the duel. She was buried where she had always longed to be: right beside her Hamilton in the Trinity Churchyard.

REUNITED *Eliza and Alexander Hamilton are buried next to each other in Manhattan's Trinity Churchyard.*

"AMERICA HAS GROWN INTO THE COUNTRY THAT HAMILTON ENVISIONED"

An interview with Ron Chernow, author of the best-selling biography that inspired the Broadway musical

BY RICHARD ZOGLIN

Historian Ron Chernow's Alexander Hamilton, *which the* New York Times *called "by far the best biography ever written about the man," was also the inspiration for the hit Broadway show. Biographer Richard Zoglin, author of* Hope: Entertainer of the Century, *talked with Chernow about Hamilton's influence on modern America, his fascinating mind and the making of his life story into a hip-hop musical.*

Q: We have fixed images of the Founding Fathers. Washington was our first president. Jefferson wrote the Declaration of Independence. All most of us know about Hamilton is that he was killed in a duel. Why is he the least understood Founding Father?

A: I think the fact that he was killed in that duel has something to do with the lack of appreciation; it robbed him of the opportunity in later years to write his own defense, or his own history of the events of the early republic. Hamilton's main political enemies were John Adams, Thomas Jefferson, James Madison and James Monroe—and I'll even throw in John Quincy Adams and Andrew Jackson for good measure. What do you notice about that list? Those were the men who were solidly in charge of American politics for many decades after Hamilton's death. Hamilton's Federalist Party had disappeared by the start of the 19th century. And if history is written by the victors, the victor during this era was the Democratic Party.

On the other hand, Hamilton had a very modern take on our economic future. He envisioned a country built on banks, corporations, stock exchanges and factories. This was a frightening and sinister vision to a lot of Americans at the time. Jefferson represented a more soothing point of view: an America of small towns and traditional agriculture. I think one reason for the eventual reappraisal of Hamilton is that America has grown into the contours of the country of his imagination, not Jefferson's. We have caught up to his prophetic vision.

Q: Hamilton is thought of as the father of our banking system and the patron saint of the Republican Party. Is that image unfair?

A: It's always very risky business to match up the political parties of the late 18th and early 19th century with the parties of today. Jefferson was a slaveholder who believed in states' rights, a weak central government, cutting taxes, strict construction of the Constitution and legislative power—that sounds rather Republican, right? Hamilton was an abolitionist who opposed states' rights, favored an activist central government, a very liberal interpretation of the Constitution and executive rather than legislative powers. That sounds much more like a modern Democrat.

WRITING HISTORY *Hamilton was "a biographer's gift" for Chernow, whose book on George Washington won a Pulitzer.*

It is more valid to say that Hamilton was a patron saint of Wall Street. In fact, when he was Treasury secretary back in the 1790s, there were only five securities traded. Three were Treasury securities created by Hamilton. The fourth were shares of the Bank of the United States, created by Hamilton. The fifth, shares of the Bank of New York—the first private bank of New York—were also created by Hamilton. So he literally had created the entire infrastructure of Wall Street.

But I feel strongly that he was a more liberal figure than people think. The image we grew up with was that Hamilton was the stooge of the plutocrats. It was a caricature, and it has undergone quite a change.

Q: **Would you say Hamilton was the smartest of the Founding Fathers?**

A: He was certainly as brilliant if not more brilliant than any of the other Founding Fathers. But that brilliance was undermined by his rather atrocious political judgment. Hamilton had a zest for political combat and a knack for winning admirers. But he had an extraordinary knack for making political enemies as well. He lacked a sense of proportion. He would very often overreact to attacks against him and only worsen matters. There's certainly a lot of needless controversy in his life.

From the time he became aide-de-camp to George Washington during the Revolutionary War, through the Constitutional Convention and his time as Treasury secretary, he was operating under Washington's guidance. If his judgment seems infallible, it's really Washington's judgment that we are witnessing. People ask me if it was a great misfortune that Hamilton never became president, and I surprise them by saying no. I think he was born to be the greatest number two in American history, because he lacked the judgment that is an indispensable quality of great presidents.

He was very ambitious, so I have no doubt that he wanted to be president. But I think he was much more suited for the role that he ended up playing. As Treasury secretary, he had the technocratic skills necessary to restore American credit, adopt state debt and create a central bank. He also was sophisticated enough to justify his activities in political terms. And as a lawyer he could argue that they were legitimized by the Constitution.

Remember: when he became Treasury secretary, the country was bankrupt; American debt was selling for 10 or 15 cents on the dollar. By the time he left office five years later, the country's credit was as good as anyone else's in the world. Most revolutionary regimes—and that's what ours was—would simply have repudiated the debt. But Hamilton felt it was important to honor it. He provided the country with an economic and financial maturity that enabled it to give the Constitution and federal government a fair test.

Q: **What do you think would have happened if he had not been killed?**

A: I think that at the time of his death, Hamilton was already wandering in the political wilderness, his political career effectively over because the Jeffersonians were solidly in control. But I think he still had great contributions to make in two areas. At the time of the duel, he was projecting a series of volumes on the history of political institutions, and he said that those books would be to the *Federalist Papers* what wine was to water, which makes me very sad that we never got to read them. Also he was one of the preeminent lawyers of his day, so I think he would have gone on to argue major cases and write distinguished briefs. So I think he would have continued to matter, even as he remained in political exile.

Q: **Did you wind up liking Hamilton?**

A: Biographers get this question all the time. Strangely enough, while I'm writing a book, I'm not really thinking about whether I like the subject or not. I'm thinking about whether I understand the person. I always think when Titian or Rembrandt made a portrait, they didn't sit there deciding if they liked the guy they were painting. Rather, they were trying to peer as deeply into that person as possible.

There's no question that I was fascinated by Hamilton, though. I admired the extraordinary number of things he did—and was appalled by his several awful lapses of judgment. He startled me on a daily basis. At every turn I found he had said something quotable or done something memorable. A biographer can ask for no more than that. Alexander Hamilton was a biographer's gift.

Q: **In my biography of Bob Hope, I felt I was making a case for him, maybe even overstating it at times. Did you feel that way with Hamilton?**

A: I thought that he had been overlooked and misunderstood, so I did feel I needed to do him justice. Not by prettying up the portrait, but by showing his gigantic list of achievements and doing my best to explain a very puzzling figure. He was a difficult character to figure out. I would love to have known much more about his parentage and formative years, the ones before he came to North America. There still is an enormous amount that we don't know and never will. He was probably the most verbal, if not the most verbose, person in American history, but there's scarcely a line in his many papers about the first third of his life, his boyhood on Nevis and St. Croix. He had a ghastly Dickensian childhood, and the way he dealt with it was to flee the Caribbean, never go back and never refer to it again. We don't have the information that helps us see him becoming Alexander Hamilton.

I think the toughest thing about spending five years with him was how hard it was on my writer's ego. Hamilton didn't have a lot of formal schooling. Still, he was one of those people who seems to have read everything, can remember everything

> *"Hamilton was a patron saint of Wall Street... But I feel strongly that he was a more liberal figure than people think."*

and is able to retrieve everything. He was a golden boy; he could write a 10,000-word memo overnight, without needing to make any changes to it when he was done. By the end of the process I felt that compared to him I was a tongue-tied idiot.

Q: Did you ever think that your book would be adapted to the screen or stage, much less be made into a hip-hop musical?
A: The book was actually optioned a few times for a feature film, but Hollywood didn't seem to know what to do with it. I found that perplexing, because I thought his is the most extraordinary story imaginable: poor, illegitimate, orphaned kid comes out of nowhere to set the world on fire. It even has standard Hollywood ingredients—sex scandal, dramatic death. And then Lin-Manuel Miranda, God bless him, picked up the book, and by the end of the second chapter, he said, in a blinding flash of inspiration he had seen the whole thing.

Q: Had you even listened to hip-hop?
A: No, I was a complete ignoramus. In fact, my first question to Lin was, can hip-hop be the vehicle for telling this kind of complex story? He said, "Ron, I'm going to educate you." He told me two things about hip-hop that I think are very important for the show's success. Number one: because of the rapidity and density of hip-hop lyrics, an enormous amount of information would be able to be packed into the show. As Lin has said, its two hours and 45 minutes is the equivalent of an advanced-placement history class. Number two: he talked about rhyme—both rhymed endings and internal rhymes. And I think one dimension of the show that hasn't gotten sufficient attention is that it carries us back to Greek drama, to Elizabethan drama—it's essentially a verse drama. I'm an old English major; I used to wonder, what did it feel like for audiences in Shakespeare's day to sit there listening to rhyme and verse? Now I know.

Q: As a consultant on the musical, did you ever reach a point when you thought Miranda was going off the rails and you had to get him back on track historically?
A: One thing that I quickly realized is that history is long, messy and complicated, and a Broadway show is short, coherent and tightly constructed. There's a tension between the two. Lin's dramatic instincts are great, and his powers of economy are extraordinary. He had to very quickly establish characters; time is telescoped and scrambled—and that I completely understood. I knew if I had been a finger-wagging pedant, the relationship would not have worked. Still, I think that my involvement, my mere presence, helped to keep him honest.

My Hamilton is very close to Lin's, but they're not identical. Nor should they be—because we have somewhat different visions of the man but, more importantly, because we were operating in different media. The Hamilton in the show is emotionally transparent and achingly human, because Lin as a dramatist has to invite us into the character's inner life. Not only could he go to places where I couldn't as a biographer, he *had* to go. Lin thought that the only way he could get us to understand Hamilton, for instance, was to hear him in conversation with his wife, Eliza. But those conversations are just plausible dramatic guesses. My Hamilton was more of his time, an 18th-century character. Lin portrayed him in a way that he couldn't have been seen by his contemporaries.

Q: How do you think Hamilton would have played today as a politician?
A: I don't think he would have survived, let alone flourished, in the current environment. He was very rational, very policy-oriented and very detailed. It's hard to imagine, in this age of tweets and sound bites, how such a massive intellect, prolific writer and verbose speaker could possibly fit in.

BROADWAY'S HIP-HOP HISTORY LESSON

Funkmaster Gil-Scott Heron once wrote that the revolution will not be televised, but he never said it wouldn't rhyme. A rapping Alexander Hamilton is this theater season's biggest draw

BY RICHARD ZOGLIN

H*AMILTON*, LIN-MANUEL MIRANDA'S new hip-hop excursion into American history, has already earned a place in Broadway history. After winning critical raves for its debut last winter at New York's Public Theater, the musical transferred to Broadway in the dog days of August, when most new shows prefer to bide their time until the splashy fall premiere season. Yet the much-buzzed-about show racked up a record-breaking advance sale of $32 million even before its August 6 opening. Since then, *Hamilton* has been Broadway's hottest ticket, pulling in better than $1.5 million per week at the box office, second only to *The Lion King*—and that's only because the Disney show is in a larger theater. Premium seats are going for as much as $1,000 apiece (though, in a small concession to democratic values, a few front-row seats for each show are on offer for $10 to patrons selected by lottery). The Obamas have been to see it, and so have Bill and Hillary Clinton, Dick Cheney, Denzel Washington, Paul McCartney and Madonna.

Rarely have the stars aligned for such an original, genre-busting show. *Hamilton* appeals to all the right constituencies, at a time when Broadway is trying to attract younger, more diverse theatergoers without alienating the reliable old-timers. It's an irreverent but respectful take on the American Revolution. It boasts a vibrant hip-hop score supplemented by old-fashioned Broadway pizzazz. And it features a multiethnic cast enacting the story of an outsider hero who was born out of wedlock in the West Indies, immigrated to New York City, and quickly became a star among the aristocrats plotting the birth of a new nation.

Miranda, creator of the Tony-winning hip-hop musical *In the Heights*, got the idea for the show after reading Ron Chernow's 2004 biography *Alexander Hamilton* while on vacation in Mexico. He was drawn to Hamilton's up-from-the-bootstraps immigrant story, which reminded him of his own Puerto Rico–born parents' experiences. He also saw, in Hamilton's headstrong personality and rhetorical prowess, links to such modern-day rappers as Tupac Shakur. It seemed only fitting that Hamilton's story be told using the music and vernacular of hip-hop—"the language of youth and

HEROIC ACT *Lin-Manuel Miranda takes center stage every night in the surprise smash he also wrote.*

energy and of rebellion," he says.

Miranda wrote the show's first song for a performance at the White House in 2009, part of an evening celebrating the American experience. His rapping tribute to Hamilton—"The 10-dollar Founding Father without a father / Got a lot farther by working a lot harder / By being a lot smarter / By being a self-starter"—got an enthusiastic reaction from the White House crowd, and Miranda set about expanding it into a full-scale musical. He did research by reading through Hamilton's voluminous correspondence and other writings; he visited numerous New York landmarks from the Revolutionary War era, as well as the Weehawken, N.J., site of Hamilton's fatal duel with Aaron Burr; and he hired Chernow himself as an adviser.

The biographer, who thought his book might make a good movie or TV miniseries but never envisioned a Broadway musical, was impressed with Miranda's determination to stay faithful to the historical record. "I said, 'You mean you want me to tell you when something is in error?' " recalled Chernow. "And he said, 'Yes, I want the historians to take this seriously.' Well, that was music to my ears. I think very often when Broadway or Hollywood does American history, they start out with the assumption that it's boring and that it has to be spiced up for the contemporary audience. Whereas Lin realized that the most dramatic way to tell this story was to stick as closely to the facts as possible."

Indeed, the show jams more real history into two hours and 45 minutes of stage time than probably any other musical in the annals of Broadway. It's all here: Hamilton's impoverished and orphaned childhood on the islands of Nevis and St. Croix; his apprenticeship as General George Washington's aide-de-camp; his marriage to the well-connected Eliza Schuyler; his role in winning support for the new U.S. Constitution and co-authorship of the *Federalist Papers*; his stint as Washington's first secretary of the Treasury and success in getting the new nation's financial house in order; the shifting political alliances and intrigues that surrounded the birthing of the American republic; and finally (inevitably) the fatal duel with Burr, his onetime friend and political rival.

"Lin said, 'I want the historians to take this seriously.' He realized that the most dramatic way to tell this story was to stick as closely to the facts as possible."

THE TRIUMPH OF *HAMILTON* is that it treats all this seriously, even as it updates Revolutionary-era history to the vernacular of today—without the jokey revisionism that marred another recent musical update of American history, *Bloody Bloody Andrew Jackson*. Instead, Miranda has crafted a full-bodied, evenhanded portrait of the era, reflecting the mix of idealism and self-interest, big ambitions and petty rivalries that animated the founding of a nation. He seems to revel in the complex, even abstruse political battles—like the compromise that Hamilton forged to get Southerners to agree to a measure allowing the federal government to assume all state debts. (In return, the Southerners got the nation's new capital placed in Virginia.) Nor does he shy from the unsavory side of Hamilton's character, notably his extramarital affair that led to blackmail and the nation's first political sex scandal.

Director Thomas Kail's high-energy production, with its ensemble of punk- and period-clad dancers, keeps even the potentially turgid passages moving along. And though the score is mostly hip-hop—so inventive and lyrically dense that it's sometimes hard to absorb in full—it also features pleasing interludes of R&B; a jazzy, up-tempo showstopper ("The Room Where It Happens"); and a catchy '60s-pop ditty in which a smug King George III taunts his unruly subjects ("You'll be back / Soon you'll see / You'll remember you belong to me . . . ").

Miranda, who also stars as Hamilton, is a dignified and surprisingly restrained presence onstage—no rock-star preening for this hip-hop master—as he sidles his way into the Revolutionary inner circle with undisguised bravado. ("Don't be shocked when your history book mentions me / I will lay down my life if it sets us free / Eventually, you'll see my ascendancy.") He is surrounded by a superb cast, especially Christopher Jackson as an imposing but very human George Washington (the most convincing Father of Our Country

A STAGED REVOLUTION Hamilton*'s cast includes (above, from left) Daveed Diggs, Okieriete Onaodowan, Anthony Ramos and playwright Lin-Manuel Miranda; below, Miranda's Hamilton bestows affection upon Phillipa Soo as Eliza.*

I've ever seen onstage) and Leslie Odom Jr. as the brooding Aaron Burr, who serves as the show's narrator and Hamilton's Javert-like nemesis. Only Jonathan Groff, as King George III, is a bit of a letdown, at least compared with Brian d'Arcy James, who had more fun with the small but showy part off-Broadway.

Is *Hamilton* a revolutionary musical? I wouldn't go that far. David Byrne's *Here Lies Love*, about the rise and fall of Imelda Marcos, had a cleaner dramatic arc and more staging originality. The sheer narrative density of *Hamilton* is also something of a handicap; too much of the history is merely told rather than dramatized. (The deadlocked presidential election of 1800, eventually decided in the House of Representatives, comes to a climax when one character simply announces, "It's a tie!")

And does the show really have to be so patronizing to the Founding Fathers who haven't been lucky enough to get a Broadway musical written about them? Thomas Jefferson (Daveed Diggs) comes across as a scheming dandy—"What'd I miss?" he sings, returning from Paris after the Revolution. James Madison (Okieriete Onaodowan) is portrayed as some sort of consumptive sphinx. (Yes, Madison had a problem with public speaking, but the man did write the Bill of Rights.) It's a bit of a wrench to see Hamilton—inventor of the nation's banking system and patron saint of Wall Street—turned into a politically correct 21st-century hero. To be sure, he was an abolitionist amid a lot of Virginia slaveholders. But he was also (the musical neglects to mention) the Founding Father who wanted the president of the United States to be elected for life.

But enough quibbles. *Hamilton* is an exciting and venturesome show, with something to please everybody: rap-music fans, American-history buffs and theater folk looking for signs of new directions for the Broadway musical. You'll walk out humming the Constitution.

Richard Zoglin is TIME*'s theater critic and the author of* Hope: Entertainer of the Century.

FACE OFF: WHY HAMILTON'S DAYS ON THE $10 BILL ARE NUMBERED

In a controversial move, the father of our financial system will be replaced, but for a good cause: to put the first woman on a Federal Reserve note

BY CHRISTOPHER MATTHEWS

ALEXANDER HAMILTON IS probably best known by the average American as the man on the $10 bill, as has been the case for generations. As the nation's first Treasury secretary, Hamilton was a natural choice to be featured on U.S. currency, and he has consistently had a place on American paper money since the U.S. government began printing it during the Civil War.

That's why it came as a shock to many when the Treasury Department announced in June 2015 that the $10 bill would be redesigned and, among other changes, would feature a woman in Hamilton's place. The Treasury is planning to issue the new note in 2020, the 100-year anniversary of the ratification of the 19th amendment, which gave women the right to vote.

Though a few women have been featured on

HARRIET TUBMAN *Conductor of the Underground Railroad*

ELEANOR ROOSEVELT *First lady, diplomat, activist*

U.S. coins and precious-metal certificates, there has never been a woman featured on a widely circulated Federal Reserve note. This sorry state of affairs motivated a group called Women on 20s to petition the White House to replace President Andrew Jackson on the $20 bill with a notable woman from the country's history. The group advocated for Jackson's ouster in particular for his role in the Indian Removal Act of 1830, which, the group wrote, "drove Native American tribes of the Southeastern United States off their resource-rich land and into Oklahoma to make room for white European settlers." These critics argue that the episode, commonly known as the Trail of Tears, should disqualify Jackson from the honor of appearing on the nation's currency.

INSTEAD OF GIVING JACKSON the boot, Treasury officials decided that it would be Hamilton whose role on U.S. currency would be diminished. Their reason: the $10 bill is the next note up for a redesign. The push to revamp the $10 bill comes from the Advanced Counterfeit Deterrence Steering Committee, an intergovernmental body chaired by the Treasury secretary that monitors counterfeiting and makes recommendations to the Treasury on how to thwart it. The change will happen at this time because the $10 bill is widely used but is produced at a lower volume than bills like the $20 note, allowing printers to transition more smoothly to the production techniques the new $10 bill will require. ($10 bills account for just 5% of notes in circulation, versus 22% for $20 bills.) One feature that will significantly change the manufacturing process is the addition of new tactile elements that will help the blind and visually impaired tell the bill apart from others.

This reasoning hasn't assuaged the irritation felt by Hamilton partisans, especially students of U.S. financial history. Following the American Revolution, Hamilton was the Founding Father who championed a vigorous financial system underwritten by the federal government. He advocated for the federal assumption of state debts following the Revolution, and he argued forcefully for the creation of the First National Bank of the U.S., actions that helped bind the nation together and establish American creditworthiness abroad.

Andrew Jackson, on the other hand, was the inheritor of a Jeffersonian suspicion of national banks and the East Coast financiers who advocated for them. Historians speculate that Jackson's antipathy for banks, and the paper money they issued, was the result of a personal land deal that went wrong. But whatever the reason for Jackson's views on monetary policy, his opposition to central banking was a primary philosophy of his presidency. He fought hard to eradicate the Second National Bank of the U.S. and was successful when its charter expired in 1836.

The results of closing the Second National Bank were devastating. The elimination of the bank helped plunge the nation into the financial Panic of 1837, which the Gilder Lehrman Institute

HOLDING ON TO HISTORY *Doug Hamilton, a direct descendant of Alexander's, is among the Americans who wish to preserve his presence on the $10 bill.*

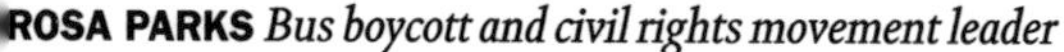

ROSA PARKS *Bus boycott and civil rights movement leader*

AMELIA EARHART *Daring transatlantic aviation pioneer*

of American History has called "the most serious economic upheaval to face the United States until the Great Depression." After Jackson killed the institution, the U.S. would go without a central bank for more than 75 years until the creation of the Federal Reserve System in 1913. This period would be marked by a series of severe financial crises, with no central authority to step in and mitigate the effects. In fact, the U.S. often had to rely on the beneficence of private actors, as it did when financier J.P. Morgan stepped in to shore up the banking system after the Panic of 1907.

In the end, the U.S. developed a financial system that hews much closer to the Hamiltonian ideal than that advocated by Jefferson and Jackson. It's therefore more than a bit ironic that Hamilton should be replaced on the face of the $10 Federal Reserve note, with Jackson's $20 note left as is. But according to the Treasury Department, the decision to place a woman on the $10 has everything to do with the need to redesign that bill for security reasons, followed closely by the belief that it's long overdue that a woman appear on U.S. currency.

THERE IS NO SHORTAGE OF qualified women who could fill Hamilton's shoes on the $10 bill. The group Women on 20s conducted its own poll, asking respondents which American woman should be the first to appear on a Federal Reserve note. The group tallied more than 600,000 votes online, with abolitionist Harriet Tubman coming in first, slightly ahead of First Lady Eleanor Roosevelt, civil rights pioneer Rosa Parks and Wilma Mankiller, the first female chief of the Cherokee Nation. Another poll, conducted by McClatchy News Service and Marist College, found Roosevelt to be America's top choice, followed by Tubman. Native American guide Sacagawea, pilot Amelia Earhart and suffragette Susan B. Anthony also received significant support.

Though Treasury secretary Jack Lew will have the final say, the Treasury Department is seeking the advice of the public through town-hall meetings, roundtable discussions and social media. As part of the outreach campaign, Treasury staff launched the hashtag #thenew10, asking the public to advocate for their choices on Facebook, Twitter and Instagram.

So despite the protestations of Hamilton fans, the father of the American financial system will no longer have a denomination of his own. And as Hamilton's portrait fades from American currency, he will take some unique traits with him. The portrait of Hamilton on the current $10 is the only left-facing one featured on Federal Reserve notes, and he is just one of two people on paper money who never served as president. (Ben Franklin is the other.) Hamilton's portrait on the $10 is also notable because it was painted by the famed American artist John Trumbull, known for his depictions of famous scenes of the Revolutionary War and the early republic. His most famous work is *The Declaration of Independence*, finished in 1818, which depicts the signing of Jefferson's famous document and is featured on the reverse side of the $2 bill.

Finally, Hamilton's removal from the $10 will also be the first time since 1928 that portraits on Federal Reserve notes were changed. That year, among other changes, the Treasury moved Hamilton from the $1,000 bill to the $10 and bumped Andrew Jackson from the $10 to the $20. The reasons these adjustments were made nearly a century ago have been lost to history. Nevertheless, the Treasury Department says that it intends to keep Hamilton on the $10 in some way, possibly with a portrait on the back of the note or in the security strip. Demoted, perhaps, but not forgotten.

Christopher Matthews, a writer at Fortune, *covers economics, real estate and financial markets.*

THE HUNK IN THE FRILLY SHIRT

Back in the day, there was no (We the) People *magazine around to name the Sexiest Man Alive. That's OK—it's clear who would have been the runaway choice*

BY BELINDA LUSCOMBE

FOUNDING FATHERS ARE LIKE OFFSPRING: secretly, everybody has a favorite. Those who love moral authority gravitate toward George Washington. Those who favor the most learned have a thing for Benjamin Franklin. For others, the turn-on is eloquence, and Thomas Jefferson rings their bell. But for those who prefer a little raw animal sexiness with their history lesson, it's hard to see past Alexander Hamilton.

Put aside that he created the federal tax system, though nothing weakens the knees like centralized revenue collection (except maybe—brace yourself—"implied powers"). Ignore too the resemblance to noted patriot Matthew McConaughey, only with Ryan Gosling's eyes. This is about more than looks. Still, if you find it hard to hand over a $10 bill, it's probably not just fiscal responsibility talking.

Clearly, Hamilton had a certain something, because historians have been swooning over the man for a while now. "He was evidently very attractive," wrote Henry Cabot Lodge in his 1882 biography of the man, "and must have possessed a great charm of manners, address, and conversation." That's 19th-century speak for "Rowrr." In historian Joseph Ellis's opinion, Hamilton was "the most brilliant, charismatic and dangerous founder of them all." Willard Sterne Randall, author of 2003's *Alexander Hamilton: A Life*, describes him as "incredibly handsome, very appealing to women and dashing," while another biographer, Ron Chernow, speaks of him as "the Elvis Presley of his time." Most recently, history buffs of a certain stripe are being enticed by T-shirts emblazoned with the slogan ALEXANDER HAMILTON: FOXIEST OF THE FEDERALISTS. (All Jefferson gets, by the way, is TREE OF LIBERTY.)

And why not? Hamilton's life arc is an unbroken narrative of seduction. Nothing tweaks the heartstrings like a sad childhood, and young Alexander's held more tragedy than *The Complete Works of William Shakespeare*. Though born into a tropical idyll as the love child of a star-crossed couple, he was soon abandoned by his father, orphaned and disinherited. And that was before he was left to fend for himself after a cousin who took him in promptly committed suicide. Impoverished, illegitimate, alone—he endured the trifecta of trauma.

Hamilton was saved by his talent. He wielded his pen like Mick Jagger used his pout, to catapult him to a whole new continent. A description of a storm that he published as a teenager grabbed the attention of benefactors who sent him off to what is now Columbia University. There, his prose moved people again, this time rallying fellow students around the revolution. Before long he was leading his literary-studies group on a daring mission to steal some cannons. It was the kind of romantic metamorphosis that only the all-time greats—Lord Byron, Ernest Hemingway—could hope to repeat.

Still, the poet-warrior vibe can take a person only so far. Hamilton supplemented his with an exotic appeal. One of eight signers of the Constitution not born in America, he brought an immigrant's mix of can-do grit, air of disreputable origins and nothing-to-lose zeal to his endeavors. When he gazed upon his young country, it was through the eyes of a foreign lover. And like a foreign lover, he helped the object of his affection see herself differently, not as a loosely affiliated union but as a single voluptuous body—nubile, fecund and ready to take on some overseas debt.

Sexiness, of course, is a hollow come-on without passion. Hamilton's fire had but two temperatures: hot and scorching. That level of ardor can get a man in trouble, and it did: Hamilton was challenged to almost a dozen affairs of honor. The noted ladies' man once dropped $60, a huge sum for someone of his means, on a ticket to one of Martha Washington's see-and-be-seen balls. His prowling did not go unnoticed; Mrs. Washington named the local tomcat after him.

And we cannot underestimate the power of his one attention-grabbing appendage. "Somebody who had a long straight nose like that," says Randall, "supposedly had a long something else." Hamilton put that something else to much use. The eight kids he had with his wife Eliza weren't enough to squelch rumors of his sleeping with his sister-in-law on the side. He definitely slept with Maria Reynolds, and that relationship ended with Hamilton writing a multi-page public confession so detailed it made Bill Clinton's Monica Lewinsky apology seem quaint.

To be fair, Hamilton's stud-muffin reputation was bolstered by his untimely death. It never hurts a hottie to die young. Hamilton was 49 when Aaron Burr mortally wounded him. That's how old stock-car legend Dale Earnhardt was at the time of his fatal crash, and how old tennis great Arthur Ashe was when he died tragically. Not for nothing, it was also the age of two Ramones when they unplugged their final amps. We envision them all as men in their rugged prime, a sweet spot between dewy innocence and wizened enfeeblement. Sure, Benjamin Franklin lived a good long time, but he's remembered as a balding hunchback.

As it should be, the greatest testament to the allure of Hamilton was offered by the widow. Though Eliza was no less a catch after her husband's death than she was when they met, she never remarried. Instead she dedicated her life to caring for orphans. Think of it as her way to ensure that the supply of Alexander Hamiltons never ran low.

Credits

FRONT COVER
Illustration for Time Books by Tim O'Brien

TITLE PAGE
Photo-illustration by Arthur Hochstein

TABLE OF CONTENTS
Mike Segar/Reuters/Corbis

INTRODUCTION
5 Niday Picture Library/Alamy
7 Arthur Hochstein

TIMELINE
(chronological order) **8** Tony Roberts/Corbis; PhotoQuest/Getty Images; The New-York Historical Society/Getty Images; Photo Stock Montage/Getty Images; Hulton Archive/Getty Images; North Wind Picture Archives/Alamy; Edward Gooch/Getty Images; MPI/Getty Images; Ed Vebell/Getty Images **9** Hulton Archive/Getty Images; Universal History Archive/UIG/Getty Images; North Wind Picture Archives/AP Images; National Archives; North Wind Picture Archives/Alamy; Kean Collection/Getty Images; MPI/Getty Images; Stock Montage/Getty Images; Imagno/Hulton Fine Art Collection/Getty Images; Ann Ronan Pictures/Print Collector/Getty Images **10** Hulton Archive/Getty Images; Corbis; MPI/Getty Images; Granger, NYC; National Archives; Granger, NYC; Universal History Archive/Getty Images; The Bureau of Engraving and Printing, U.S. Government; Library of Congress; Kean Collection/Getty Images; Granger, NYC **11** Granger, NYC; GraphicaArtis/Getty Images; GraphicaArtis/Getty Images; Granger, NYC; Brown Brothers; Granger, NYC; Classic Image/Alamy; Patti McConville/Alamy

EARLY LIFE
12 George H.H. Huey/age fotostock/Getty Images **15** Don Hebert/Stockbyte/Getty Images **16** Archive Farms/Getty Images **17** Library of Congress **18** (from top) Library of Congress; Granger, NYC **19** robertjhill/RooM/Getty Images

STUDENT
21 (top) North Wind Picture Archives/Alamy; (bottom, from left) Fine Art Images/Heritage Images/Getty Images; DeAgostini/Getty Images; Painting/Alamy; DeAgostini/Getty Images **22** Chronicle/Alamy **23** Superstock/Getty Images

SOLDIER
25 North Wind Picture Archives/AP Photo
26 North Wind Picture Archives/Alamy
27 FineArt/Alamy

MARRIED LIFE
29 Granger, NYC **30** Granger, NYC **31** (from left) Stock Montage/Getty Images; Granger, NYC

SIX FACTS ABOUT HAMILTON
32 (clockwise) DEA Picture Library/Getty Images; Universal History Archive/Getty Images; DEA Picture Library/Getty Images; Kean Collection/Getty Images; Stock Montage/Getty Images **33** (from left) Jono David; Wikimedia Commons **34** (from top) Granger, NYC; Bequest of William McIlvaine, 1901/Wikimedia Commons **35** (from left) Clarence Holmes Photography/Alamy; Granger, NYC

THE FEDERALIST PAPERS
37 Hulton Archive/Getty Images **38** National Archives **39** (from left) DEA Picture Library/Getty Images; GraphicaArtis/Getty Images **41** Bettmann/Corbis **42** Granger, NYC

RIVALRY
44 Lee Snider/Photo Images/Corbis
45 age fotostock/Alamy **47** Illustration by Barry Blitt for TIME **49** Library of Congress

THE *NEW YORK POST*
51 From New York Post (March 16), © 1993 NYP Holding, Inc. All rights reserved. Used by permission and protected by the Copyright Laws of the United States. The printing, copying, redistribution, or retransmission of this content without express written permission is prohibited.

THE BANKING SYSTEM
53 Illustration by C.F. Payne **54** Stock Montage/Getty Images **55** Granger, NYC **56** Ron Rovtar Photography/Alamy **57** Kevork Djansezian/Getty Images

HAMILTON'S LETTERS
59 Granger, NYC **60** (from top) Kean Collection/Getty Images; Granger, NYC **61** (clockwise) Photo12/UIG via Getty Images; Granger, NYC; Kean Collection/Getty Images; Hulton Archive/Getty Images **62** (from top) Archive Photos/Getty Images; Corbis **63** (from top) Stefano Giovannini, stefanogiovannini.com; Granger, NYC

NEW YORK CITY HOME
65 (from top) Stefano Giovannini, stefanogiovannini.com; Library of Congress
66 (from top) Harry Warnecke/NY Daily News Archive/Getty Images; Andrew Henderson/The New York Times/Redux
67 (clockwise) Joshua Bright/The New York Times/Redux; Terese Loeb Kreuzer/Alamy; Stefano Giovannini, stefanogiovannini.com

THE DUEL
68 North Wind Picture Archives/Alamy
70 (from left) Granger, NYC; Stocktrek Images, Inc./Alamy **71** Granger, NYC
72 Beth J. Harpaz/AP Photo **73** Granger, NYC **74** Collection of the New-York Historical Society **75** (from top) Keith Meyers/The New York Times/Redux; Chronicle/Alamy

THE GOOD WIFE: ELIZA
77 Granger, NYC **78** (from left) Granger, NYC; Universal History Archive/Getty Images; Interim Archives/Getty Images **80** (from top) Granger, NYC; Photo12/UIG/Getty Images
81 Arthur Hochstein

INTERVIEW WITH RON CHERNOW
83 Nina Subin **85** Harland Sund/Getty Images

THE HAMILTON MUSICAL
87–89 Joan Marcus (3)

A NEW $10 BILL
90–91 Illustration by Arthur Hochstein; $10 bill by Nick Fielding/Alamy **92–93** (top) Illustrations by TIME; $10 bill by Nick Fielding/Alamy (4); (from left) Ann Ronan Pictures/Print Collector/Getty Images; Stock Montage/Getty Images; Don Cravens/The LIFE Images Collection/Getty Images; The Seattle Times/JR Partners/Getty Images; (bottom) Mitch Stacy/AP Photo

HAMILTON THE HUNK
94 Illustration by Roberto Parada

CREDITS/MASTHEAD
96 iStock by Getty Images

TIME

Editor Nancy Gibbs
Creative Director D.W. Pine
Director of Photography Kira Pollack

ALEXANDER HAMILTON

A Founding Father's Visionary Genius—and His Tragic Fate

Editor Neil Fine
Designer Arthur Hochstein
Photo Editor Lizabeth Ronk
Writers Richard Beeman, Sarah Begley, Ron Chernow, John Ferling, Joanne B. Freeman, Daniel S. Levy, Belinda Luscombe, Christopher Matthews, Courtney Mifsud, Lily Rothman, John Sedgwick, Ellen Tumposky, Richard Zoglin
Copy Editor Joseph McCombs
Editorial Production David Sloan

Time Inc. Books

Publisher Margot Schupf
Associate Publisher Allison Devlin
Vice President, Finance Terri Lombardi
Executive Director, Marketing Services Carol Pittard
Executive Director, Business Development Suzanne Albert
Executive Publishing Director Megan Pearlman
Associate Director of Publicity Courtney Greenhalgh
Assistant General Counsel Andrew Goldberg
Assistant Director, Special Sales Ilene Schreider
Assistant Director, Production Susan Chodakiewicz
Senior Manager, Sales Marketing Danielle Costa
Senior Manager, Category Marketing Bryan Christian
Brand Manager Katherine Barnet
Associate Brand Manager Krystal Venable
Associate Production Manager Amy Mangus
Associate Prepress Manager Alex Voznesenskiy
Assistant Project Manager Hillary Leary

Editorial Director Stephen Koepp
Art Director Gary Stewart
Director of Photography Christina Lieberman
Editorial Operations Director Jamie Roth Major
Senior Editor Alyssa Smith
Assistant Art Director Anne-Michelle Gallero
Copy Chief Rina Bander
Assistant Managing Editor Gina Scauzillo
Editorial Assistant Courtney Mifsud

Special thanks to: Allyson Angle, Brad Beatson, Jeremy Biloon, Ian Chin, Rose Cirrincione, Pat Datta, Nicole Fisher, Alison Foster, Joan L. Garrison, Erika Hawxhurst, Kristina Jutzi, Jean Kennedy, Seniqua Koger, Amanda Lipnick, Melissa Presti, Kate Roncinske, Babette Ross, Dave Rozzelle, Kelsey Smith, Larry Wicker

Published by Time Books, an imprint of Time Inc. Books
225 Liberty St., New York, NY 10281

We welcome your comments and suggestions about Time Books. Please write to us at: Time Books, Attention: Book Editors, P.O. Box 62310, Tampa, FL 33662-2310 If you would like to order any of our hardcover Collector's Edition books, please call us at 800-327-6388, Monday through Friday, 7 a.m.–9 p.m. Central Time.

Made in the USA
Lexington, KY
22 February 2016